GROTZ'S

DECORATIVE
COLLECTIBLES
PRICE GUIDE

Books by George Grotz:

FROM GUNK TO GLOW

THE FURNITURE DOCTOR

THE NEW ANTIQUES

ANTIQUES YOU CAN DECORATE WITH

INSTANT FURNITURE REFINISHING

STAINING AND REFINISHING UNFINISHED FURNITURE
AND OTHER NAKED WOODS

DECORATING FURNITURE WITH A LITTLE CLASS

THE ANTIQUE RESTORER'S HANDBOOK

THE CURRENT ANTIQUE FURNITURE STYLE & PRICE GUIDE

THE FUN OF REFINISHING FURNITURE

GROTZ'S 2ND ANTIQUE FURNITURE STYLE & PRICE GUIDE

GROTZ'S DECORATIVE COLLECTIBLES PRICE GUIDE

GROTZ'S

DECORATIVE

COLLECTIBLES

PRICE GUIDE

Edited by GEORGE GROTZ

1983

DOLPHIN BOOKS

DOUBLEDAY & COMPANY, INC., GARDEN CITY, NEW YORK

Library of Congress Cataloging in Publication Data

Grotz, George.
Grotz's Decorative collectibles price guide.

1. Collectibles—United States—Catalogs.
I. Title. II. Title: Decorative collectibles
price guide.
AM303.G76 1983   790.1'32   82-45288
ISBN 0-385-17870-0

Contents

Contents

Preface: Collectibles
You Can Decorate With

Collectibles are small but visually exciting pieces that speak to us of other places, other times. And while they usually only sit on tables or hang on walls, they invariably "liven up the place" and make good conversation pieces.

For this first edition of this Decorative Collectibles Price Guide, over 2,500 objects were originally photographed. From these the present 900 and some were selected as being representative of the most colorful things that are currently available at the better flea markets and country auctions. Thus many more objects can be judged by comparison.

The prices given are those you should pay at a good flea market or a country auction in New England and in the states down the East Coast to North Carolina — which, after all, is where 90 percent of our antiques and quality collectibles come from. So these are "source" prices, and if you live west of the source area, you naturally have to add the cost of transportation. And if you are buying from a dealer, you also have to accept his making at least enough on the sale to cover his overhead. But since anyone can go to the sources — and an awful lot of people do — these prices seem to be the logical ones on which to establish relative values.

But that doesn't mean that the prices given in this book are necessarily the ones that were being asked when these objects were observed and photographed. There are too many variables for that — such as ridiculously low prices at an auction because it rained that day. Or a high price at a flea market because the seller is trying to find how much a piece is really worth by getting offers. Or if the seller is a bargainer, and always starts high. Or if the object is "hot," or a fake, and the seller wants to get rid of it in a hurry. Lots of things.

So to cut through all that confusion, the prices given in this book are estimates of value given to me by seasoned auctioneers through whose hands similar objects are passing day after day. Of course, there's still always room for argument . . . but that's what makes life interesting!

Happy hunting!
George Grotz

The Brimfield
Experience
or, where the
collectibles come from

About sixty miles due west of Boston lies a wide alluvial (means flat) valley. In the middle of it stands a classic New England town — big white church, a common shaded by giant trees and surrounded by Colonial homes with their old barns and carriage houses standing guard just behind them. It is the village of Brimfield, Massachusetts. A quiet place most of the year, the kind of a place where if you have nothing to do, you've found the place not to do it in.

But three times a year — once in the spring, once in the summer, and once in the fall — something happens. Something really happens. For three times a year two thousand antique dealers — their trucks and vans packed to overflowing with their merchandise — converge on the sleepy little town from all over New England, the near South, and the Midwest to hold a joyous powwow and sell everything they have brought to each other at obviously trade or wholesale prices.

And this is no flea market. You will find no used toasters. These are all serious antique dealers who come as much to buy stock as to sell it. They are there to do business — almost all of them with five to twenty-five thousand dollars' worth of small antiques and collectibles packed in corrugated cartons. Just for a rough estimate let's multiply $10,000 by two thousand dealers — that's twenty million dollars' worth of small, portable antiques and collectibles! Wow!

The way it works is that five farms bordering the highway that runs through the center of the valley have been converted into exhibition grounds with grids of gravel-topped "streets" along which the dealers rent small plots in which to park their vehicles and set up folding tables groaning with their leftovers of the past.

The show lasts a week. But it doesn't all start at once. The traffic jam would be impossible to handle. Instead, the openings of the five farms are staggered through seven days until at the end of the week everybody is set up, as the saying goes.

And a good time is had by all because it is fun to camp out in your van and cook on your Coleman stove for a few days where you can meet old friends and sit around sipping coffee in the sun and swapping lies about how much money you are making. Sure beats working, as the saying goes.

One day I was talking to a dealer from Philadelphia when a young man walked by with a couple of empty Coke cans in his hand — obviously looking for a trash can. The dealer spoke up to him, saying, "Here, I'll throw them away for you." And as the dealer took the cans from

9

the young man the dealer's wife said to him, "Hey, honey, I thought we were here to sell trash, not to collect it."

So Brimfield is the essential place for you to find the kind of objects that are illustrated in this book. And while it is basically a dealers' exchange or marketplace, everybody with money is certainly welcome. As to the exact dates of the three Brimfield weeks, they vary, but they are basically the second weeks in May, July, and September. To get the exact dates just ask your friendly local antiques dealer, who will look them up for you in his current copy of *The Newtown Bee* or *The Maine Antique Digest,* the trade tabloids of the antiques business. Maybe you can go along with him — and his wife. Can you imagine it — four thousand people cooking on Coleman stoves in one alluvial valley!

GROTZ'S

DECORATIVE
COLLECTIBLES
PRICE GUIDE

Advertising

Advertising poster for the RCA Victor trademark— "His Master's Voice." Framed,
$175

Very good artwork makes this framed poster a winner. Especially good for decorating offices of business big shots. Sells for about **$100**, but you can turn a quick buck by selling it to an interior decorator for
$175

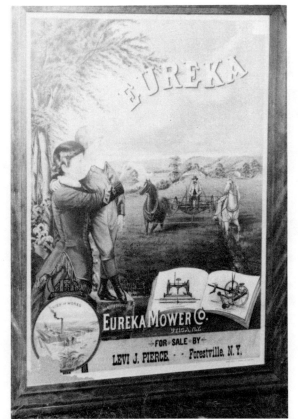

Advertising poster, framed,
$50–$75

Yes, there was Pepsi-Cola back in the olden times, even if it wasn't as ubiquitous as Coca-Cola. And this lovely lady on a lithographed tin tray goes for
$45–$55

Good old advertising tray. Anything with portraits in costume goes best. Hung on the wall of a restaurant or game room,
$50–$60

Animals and dogs acting like people is a joke some people go nuts over—especially in Merrie Olde England. Should bring **$125** even here. Eighteen inches long.

Framed poster ad with lots of faces, about 30 inches high. Worth
$35–$50

14

Enamelware plaques like these were attached to outside of office buildings to tell what went on inside. A really zooming collectible, hardly noticed ten years ago. This one is now up to **$350**. But the pictorial interest is so great it is a terrific investment. Should be **$700** in two years.

Set of three lobby sheets advertising *Traffic in Souls*, a thriller of the early thirties. Worth **$60–$80** apiece, but in this unusual set about **$300** for the set of three. Many are on display at the Goyette Museum in Peterboro, New Hampshire.

Really coming into vogue are all cigarette items such as this framed Lucky Strike ad, which does its best to imply that smoking cigarettes will help you reduce. Only **$40**, and a comer.

Close-up of the advertising message on Lucky Strike ad whose headline is "When tempted . . . reach for a Lucky instead."

AVOID THAT FUTURE SHADOW

by refraining from over-indulgence

We do not represent that smoking **Lucky Strike** Cigarettes will cause the reduction of flesh. We do declare that when tempted to do yourself too well, if you will "Reach for a **Lucky**" instead, you will thus avoid over-indulgence in things that cause excess weight and, by avoiding over-indulgence, maintain a trim figure.

Detail of the artwork on a 1930s beer tray. Ones as good as this worth **$60–$75**

Base reads "HUNTER—first over the Bar." It's a whiskey. It's a pun. Advertising statuette, 18 inches high. Done from a photograph of George Alberghetti, who got paid $200 to jump. Statuette worth **$200** today. Made of hollow-cast white metal, which is far better than plaster.

"Ma" Bell goes over big in game rooms, so in spite of the plethora of these old telephone-booth signs they go for around
$50

These enamelware signs are made of colored glass applied in powder form and baked onto metal—same as the pots. This one was going for **$160**. People who own restaurants can't resist them—probably because they clean so easily.

Fifteen-inch-high hollow-cast white metal camel in rich colors of paint. With lighter on his hump because he advertised Turkish cigarettes called Red Kamels. So decorative that any interior decorator would give you **$250** for it.

Two-and-a-half-foot-wide box used to sell seeds in the country store. New box every year, since seeds were shipped in it. Lots of them around, but so colorful they are worth **$60–$75** if label is in good condition.

Everything with Moxie on it sells well because it tasted so bad that only New Englanders could punish themselves by drinking it—Puritan heritage, you know. Framed ad here **$125**. Rare Moxie toys like this car are worth **$650–$800**.

Orange-Crush brings back memories of our innocence. Great for parties in the game room.
$100

But here is cultural art in this colorful porcelain Cherry Smash dispenser. This one has lost its chrome-plated pump cover, so only worth **$150**. With the pump, **$225**.

18

A dull and dopey tray, but still worth about **$20** if you met your sweetheart there while selling hot dogs. There's *somebody* who wants *anything*.

Nice, big, lithographed-on-tin sign about 3 feet long used to sell tours of Europe. This one is pretty late, as it shows the *Queen Mary*. Worth **$150–$200**. Older ones are worth as much as twice that.

Mr. Peanut is worth twice what other advertising symbols are in any form. This set of lithographed tin peanut serving dishes, though small—center dish is only 6 inches across—goes for over **$100**

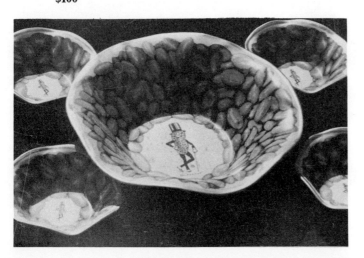

Cardboard calendar given away by the local grocer. Often printed in kaleidoscopic color in Germany like so many postcards. In perfect condition for framing, **$75–$100** since cat lovers will buy anything with cats in it.

Nice ceramic ashtray and match holder made of German china with ad flashed onto porcelain. Used on tables of restaurants.
$35

Glass humidor for cigars with an unusually colorful decal-type transfer on it. Rubber air seal that fits on top is usually gone. Worth
$65–$100

Thirty-inch-wide cardboard advertising poster for soap. Only cardboard, but this one has everything going for it —the eagle, stars and stripes, American Family. With all that Americana— at least
$110

American Indian Artifacts

Rag-and-yarn doll with original homespun material, quite old. An authentic artifact.
$225

Hopi Cotina doll, a rainmaker's doll. Baked clay, 6 inches tall.
$125

Grouping of Indian arrowheads. From **$5–$40**, depending on shape and size.

Pottery jar, about 15 inches high, soft
faded colors, perhaps 100 years old,
$500–$700 each.

Indian doll made of carved wood, soft
muted colors, 12 inches high. Festival
doll. **$250**. If larger, **$400**.

Beadwork moccasins of deer hide.
$125–$150

Indian trade doll or "Railway Doll,"
because they were made for selling
down at the train stations to the
passengers passing through. Good
baked clay face on this one.
$175

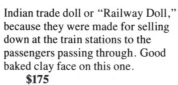

Three little dolls in a beautifully done pouch. Fabric faces in mint condition.
$450

Early settler (in the West) dolls. Center squaw in hide dress with carved wood head, **$275**. Stocking-head dolls on either side, **$150**.

Ornate deer-hide clothing on doll with washed-away face.
$250

23

Art Deco

Hollow-cast white-metal table lamp with bronzed finish that you could usually win at a carnival in the early 1900s, maybe up to 1935. The low-wattage lamp was behind a piece of cloth pasted in the window to give a soft lovin' glow to the bedroom on Montego Street. A boudoir lamp. Worth **$75–$125**

Pair of lamps made of orange-and-red slag glass with naked white-metal ladies supporting them. Bronzed. Maxfield Parrish period, but the nudes are fatter than those the great illustrator preferred. At least **$200** for the pair.

Simple production-made bureau lamp given away with a bedroom furniture set in 1920s and early '30s. Dressing table lamp. Only **$35** out in Brimfield, but in New York City somebody will pay up to **$135** for it. I wish I had bought it!

24

Glass global lamp on white-metal base with dancing girls to spice up lonely nights in your game room.
$125

White-metal lamp with the wandering minstrel and a lady piano player. Actually, both figures are ladies.
$125–$150

A work of art, hand-punched into a brass casing, this is the base of a large table lamp. Betty Boop is terrific, and this is the best of Art Deco.
$650. Worth **$1,100**, or more

A glass cube lamp of the modernistic school of the late '20s. Kind of pathetic, but currently around **$35**, and will climb. The world is full of people with more money than taste.

Another white-metal lamp base, but with a very good subject having special appeal to those rich businessmen who are golfers. Bobby Jones?
$250

Lamp with a low-wattage electric bulb behind a red cloth in the fireplace. Mostly went on top of the big old box-on-stand radios. A night-light for the living room. A carnival prize.
$85

Terrific Art Deco cigarette box in bronzed white metal with a lot of humor to it. Box lined with heavy pieces of dark glass. The nature forms on the base are an inheritance from Art Nouveau, which this happy stuff mocked. 1920s and early '30s.
$175–$200

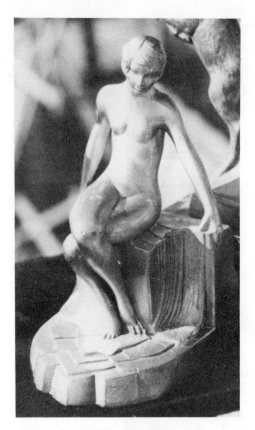

Another pair of bookends without much chest in the manner of Maxfield Parrish, New Hampshire's gift to the world of art. Bronzed white metal. Just another imitation of the real thing, but still worth **$75**. (The real thing in bronze and signed would be in the $800s.)

From 1930s this imitation of the famous Maxfield Parrish flat-chested nudes. A pair of bookends.
  $85

Detail of Art Deco cigarette box showing sexy lady to be smoking a cigar.

Detail of airplane smoking stand.

If this looks like a floor-lamp base, that's only because it probably was. But that is a very good airplane on top of it that makes this piece worth almost anything you want to pay for it. It was seen at **$250** in Brimfield—a steal.

Nice ashtray stand made by the same people who used to make standing floor lamps. The horse is bronzed cast iron. But the important thing is that the stand still has its glass dish. Without the dish **$25**. With it, **$100**.

Coffee-table cigarette lighter in chrome-plated cast iron. Lighter pops up when you turn the propeller. An easy **$125** if you have one in the attic.

Calendar art of the 1930s that Dad used
·to hang in the garage.
$35

Paperweight, white-metal clock with
some really nieve sculptured ladies. If
you have a warped sense of humor you
will pay **$125** for this out in the wilds of
Rettingers—sell it for double in New
York City.

"Roosevelt at the wheel for a New
Deal." Made in the 1930s with an electric clock in the wheel. Without the
clock **$125**. With original or any other
electric clock fitted in, add another **$50**.

Very nice night-table clock transitional piece between Art Nouveau and Art Deco. (The vines are integral to the legs —but it is a white-metal "novelty" design, with the thoughtful lady definitely a Deco idea.) Sells for
$150–$175

Homely-looking object, but definitely of the Art Deco period—typical of the bad taste of the Sessions clock once coveted by company executives. Ugly as it is, it can go for
$100

King of the carnival prizes was this hollow-cast horse and electric clock in the days when electric clocks were wonderments. And still being made. But this one is old and pretty good.
$65

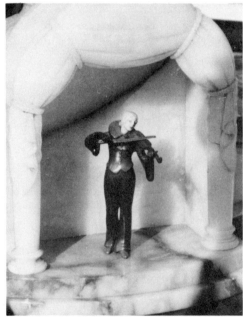

Very nice Art Nouveau-into-Deco. Metal body with carved ivory-type composition head. The rest all marble. Very romantic and sophisticated. Eight inches high. A **$350** object.

The stripes are on the back of the glass, with uncoated oval left to reveal Deanna Durbin or whoever. A ten-cent-store item that is now worth **$15** for nostalgia.

Wall lamp basically found in public buildings—like the famous Chrysler Building in New York City. Often in lobbies and corridors of hotels. So if that is the part of your life you want to remember, you can get these for
$75–$100

Pair of bronze wolfhounds mounted on marble, a 15-inch-wide mantelpiece decoration. And not bad. **$175**. Not good either. Better dogs would make it worth much more.

Art Nouveau

A pair of vases in the Art Nouveau manner, which means that lines found in nature are utilized in designing the object. Lots of vines, flower decoration, swoops, and swirls. And while the idea may sound a little simple-minded, the results are always lovely. These white-metal, silvered, and antique-glazed bud vases—**$175** for the pair.

Pair of vases about 10 inches high. Glass, sprayed with bronze-colored paint. With the paint cleaned off with a little lacquer thinner, **$90** for the pair.

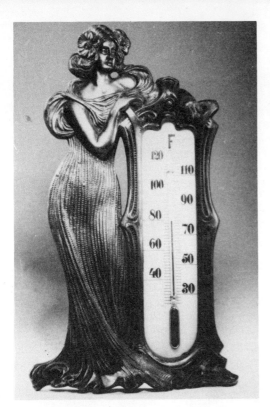

A lady to make your temperature go up, 10 inches high, cast iron, bronze finish, head and neck golden, dress reddish, and how they did that I haven't the slightest idea.
$150

Detail of thermometer lady dreaming of times gone by before her head started shrinking.

White-metal pitcher with gorgeous golden and green glazed finish. About 10 inches high. Use of the woman's body as the handle, the spout in the shape of a leaf, are both pure Art Nouveau. A signed casting, worth around **$350**. (If it was an original Tiffany product, it would be more like **$3,500**!)

Detail of lady acting as a pitcher handle.

An iron casing with an electroplated bronze finish, about 6 inches wide, and designed for use as an ashtray. To Art Nouveau designers, the lines of nature that were most appealing were those of the female body. *Vive la différence!* For this body,
$35

Back of beautiful lady ashtray, showing that it was given away to people who toured the Bethlehem Foundry and Machine Company out there in Pennsylvania.

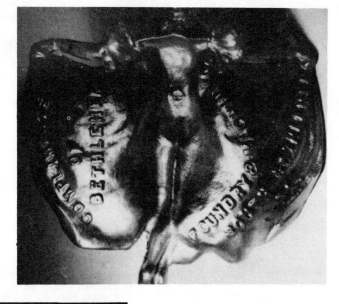

Statuette of resting ballerina. White metal, bronzed casting. A little on the Deco side.
$125

Five-inch-high, very French looking, hand-decorated plaster—part of a toilet set from the '20s.
$60

34

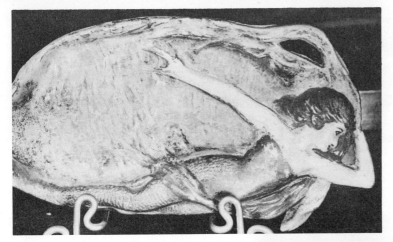

Polychrome-painted, cast-iron ashtray with a real mermaid, 7 inches long.
$75

German porcelain which needs a new pearl glued to the bathing beauty's oyster shell. A seaside souvenir of a long-past happy time for someone. Ah, how the summers of life fly by! Bye, bye.
$45–$70

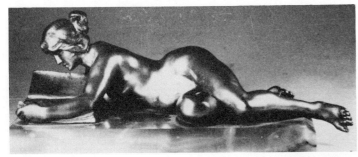

Eight-inch-long genuine solid-brass woman reading a book on a green-marble base. Very realistic rendering of a woman's body that is typical of Victorian artists. Although of the Art Nouveau period, this is more an art object than merely the product of a style. And because it is also sexy,
$1,100

Detail of lady reading a book in her realistic buff.

35

Nice little cut-glass powder jar with a sterling silver top. Signed Libby on the bottom, worth **$150–$175.** Unsigned **$50** less.

The simple application of vines to something is not the essential idea of Art Nouveau style, so this is really just a second-rate piece of around the same period. Leaded-glass shade is merely a pattern—as opposed to being in the shape of pears and such. Yet people will pay **$1,500** and up for this mediocre sort of thing because it is at least a third cousin of Tiffany's work. I hate it.

Detail of lamp base with vines.

36

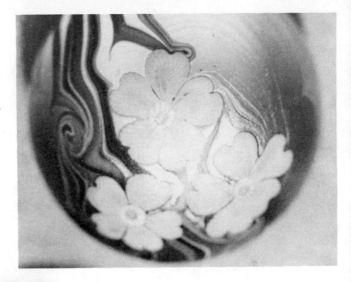

Paperweight with flowers in the Art Nouveau manner. But too crude to be of any real value. Still . . .
$175

Demure young lady with realistically small breastworks that is really a reproduction of a work of art, French Victorian influence. Lamps like these were often given to people who had their houses electrified, but this is an especially good example. Twenty-four inches high. A great investment at the mere **$350** such lamps are now selling for. Loveliness has some importance, too, you know.

Detail of French *nymphette* lamp.

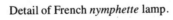

37

Similar to a small clock shown in the Art Deco section, this one moves into Art Nouveau on the basis of its legs being more viny. Also more graceful. The clocks are interchangeable on most of these pieces. Fourteen inches high, this object is in the **$200–$250** class.

Six-inch-high cheap German china, early gift-shoppe shelf piece. Nice colors.
$75

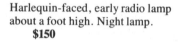

Harlequin-faced, early radio lamp about a foot high. Night lamp.
$150

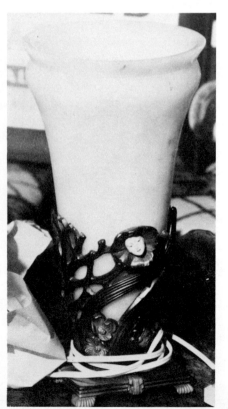

Somehow this 8-inch-high Chinaware object comes across with a mandarin flavor. With leafy vine handles and the lady with the usual Victorian hairdo, it's a vase for your sideboard.
$125

Dog-bone radiator cap so you can get it on really tight—fits on almost any car. An accessory. Also has thermometer inside to tell you when you are about to boil over.
$125

Another motometer with a thermometer in it.
$50–$75

Ho, ho. The hood ornament of an old Pontiac automobile just after the Second World War. Had a little bulb in it that lit up when your parking lights were on. If this is your piece of cake, you will have to pay **$125** to cut the mustard.

Another Pontiac radiator cap from mid-'30s. Chrome-plated, and worth **$75–$100**

Aviation

This superb piece looks like folk art at first—wonderful weathering. But circular engine and prop are castings. Must originally have been a toy or whirligig. About 14 inches long, and everyone who looked at it out in Brimfield agreed that it was well worth **$500**. Sold for **$450**.

Second view of weathered airplane with circular motor—i.e., very early.

For comparison to preceding weathered model, note motor on Lindbergh's *Spirit of St. Louis*. This is an unsigned Underwood & Underwood print, part of a series taken for use on the covers of sheet music celebrating the famous flight. But this shot was not used, so it may be a very rare print. An 11" x 14" blowup. Maybe
$1,100

Toy cast-iron airplane whose wheels drove the prop by means of a rubber belt. A **$175** treasure.

Hard-rubber wheels on a cast-iron airplane.
$125

Toy tri-motor, 20-inch wingspan, that you could taxi around the field.
$125

Early tri-motor with casting of circular engine and rubber wheels still intact. Eighteen inches wide.
$250

41

Small cast-lead toy—3 inches long.
Common at
$22

World War II cardboard device for spot-
ting American aircraft by their silhou-
ettes. Very colorful.
$50

Miniature lead airplanes, trucks, and
cars selling from
$12–$25

42

BEWARE OF FAKES—During the 1930s thousands of exact copies of mechanical cast-iron banks were made for use in a promotional campaign for an encyclopedia. When these have been skillfully distressed, only an expert can tell them from the real thing. They have slightly sharper edges on the bottom, faintly different colors, and chip with a larger flake.

Mammy-doll bank about 5 inches tall. Still bank, cast iron, all decoration worn off. **$75**. With original paint intact, **$150**. Prices on all "Black-related" items are probably inflated due to the idea that they should rise in value, a reasoning that is obvious to even those of the meanest intelligence.

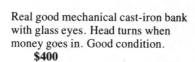

Real good mechanical cast-iron bank with glass eyes. Head turns when money goes in. Good condition. **$400**

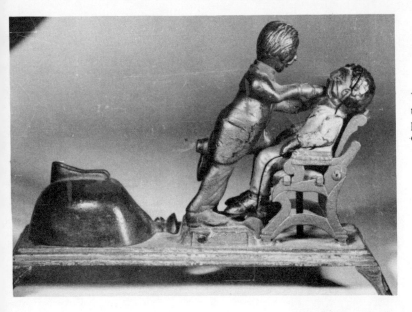

Very rare mechanical bank. "The Dentist." Push the coin in, and the dentist pulls a tooth. Even with paint half worn off, this goes for an easy
$1,200

Well-worn but authentic Punch and Judy bank. Depending on the condition of *original* paint job, these sell for from
$350–$650

Bank called "Creedmore" shoots a penny into the tree when you press the man's foot to release a spring mechanism. Nice old color. **$450**. Anybody know *why* it is called "Creedmore"?

Jonah carries coins into whale's mouth.
$450–$550

Authentic mother eagle feeding chick.
Not reproduced.
$550

Suspicious-looking clown bank with
dog that jumps through hoop. However,
even the fakes sell for good prices. And
if you can't tell the difference . . . ?
Either way, this bank is worth a chance
at
$225

Football kicker. A cast-iron toy that
kicks a cast-iron football. With football
$225. Without . . . make one out of
wood or something.

45

Life-size photo of lithographed tin dime bank given out by savings banks. Hold onto your hat, but all Popeye items go for wild prices. This bank goes for
$30

Still cast-iron elephant bank with some original green paint. Circus elephant.
$35

Nice little house bank about 3 inches tall. Screws together.
$40

46

Skyscraper and bank with fourteen floors and a Louis Sullivan look, which goes over big with architects.
$125

Strange, turreted building bank of cast iron.
$125

Lithographed tin dime bank.
$25

47

Baskets

Split-ash basket with stationary handle. Similar to chair seating. Going up fast. **$75–$100**

Goose-down basket out of split ash, missing its cover but still worth **$150**. Twenty-two inches tall.

Two split-ash baskets with stationary handles. One inside is a reproduction dyed brown with coffee. But that doesn't seem to make any difference with baskets since they are made exactly the same way the old ones were. It's **$45** for the little one; **$80** for the big one.

48

Vintage 1930 L.L. Bean picnic basket of split ash now going over big as hand-bags. Good ice-coolers if lined with zinc. Either way,
$35–$45

Genuine Indian sweet-grass basket from New Mexico.
$25–$35

Indian good-luck sign decorates this handwoven basket with nice rim handles. A foot in diameter.
$50–$60

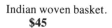

Indian woven basket.
$45

49

Boat Models

Fully rigged ship model with a little lifeboat on the side containing two carved men, fitted in a cradle for mantelpiece display. Nice; old work and rigging in good shape. Over 2 feet long.
$400

Glass-encased boat model in good condition.
$225

"Needs work" specials like this one go for around **$35** if all the parts are there.

Primitive submarine made by Grandpa.
$12

Hollowed-out piece of wood from the
Victorian era, colorful, 8 inches long.
Quality work. Reminds you of a Sar-
gent rural painting.
$35

Very primitive ship in a bottle that has
far more charm than an intricate one.
Eight inches long. Can be picked up
cheap as just another boat in a bottle.
Say, **$25–$35**. But then you can sell it
as primitive art for **$145–$165**.

Three feet long, this model has a brass
steam engine in it. Very Victorian
model of a launch. Even if it doesn't
work, it's worth at least
$400

Hobbyist's special. Nice sail rings around mast. Buy for **$45**, fix, and sell for **$175**.

Complete, complex, and authentic in proportions.
$350–$400

Side-wheeler done for the captain while the boat was being built.
$500–$700

52

Coastal steamer ready for restoration.
About
$125

Nice two-masted sloop. (Both masts
same height—rare.) Great for some
banker's office. Nice natural-wood
colors.
$450

Homemade, crudely done, but very interesting tugboat. Heads toward primitive art because of the nieve interpreta-
tion of a tugboat's lines. Typically un-
derpriced at **$150**. Two feet long, and
could go for **$450** or more in New York
City to an art lover—maybe **$650**.
A real worth-what-you-can-get-for-it
object.

53

About 2½ feet long, crude sheet-metal model of an ocean liner. As an inferior boat model, **$125**. As primitive art, **$350**.

Shadow-box model with painted background. As model, **$350**. But can anyone miss that this is great primitive art? As such, an easy **$750** or more.

Mechanical, spring-driven, with long-lasting clock movement, this model was made in England as an expensive Victorian toy that came over here in the 1920s.
  $850

54

Books, Magazines, and Cards

A hundred pages of Gibson girls and their friends in 11″ x 14″ format—all worthy of framing—is a good buy at **$125**

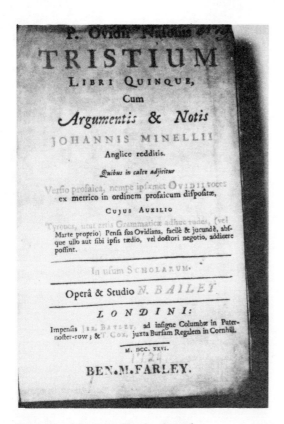

Two-color title page of leather-bound book dated 1724 pushes price of this particular book up to **$35**. A translation of Ovid.

Title page of an early Webster's Unabridged Dictionary, which is available for only **$15** because binding is only cardboard.

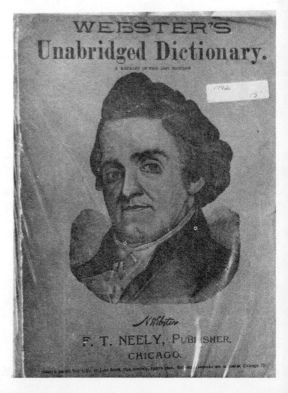

Old leather binding on this book makes it worth
$10

Elbert Hubbard-era gift booklets of an inspiring nature. Two for
$15

Old copy of *McCall's Magazine*. Covers great for framing. Available for from
$3–$15

Piggy walks out by the Seaside.

Cards like this 11″ x 14″ card printed in
England sell for **$20–$25** each.

Very frameable.
$25

Bunny playing Leap-Frog at home.

Christmas card in full color, printed in
Germany.
$10

A merry Christmas to You

Bottles

Broken-off pontil shows that bottle was blown by hand—making such bottles worth in the **$40**-and-up class.

This is the hand-blown bottle, of which you have already seen the broken-off base. Notice crooked neck.

Drugstore bottle, made for a local druggist who applied his own labels. That is, not a mass-produced patent medicine bottle. About
$25–$35

Bottom that shows bottle was blown into a brass or sand mold, making it worth around
$15

Patent medicine bottle that once contained Hamlin's Wizard Oil that cured anything. Originally had a cork stopper.
$5–$7

·"Soothing Syrup" bottle, 5 inches long, blown in a mold. Coruscating pinks and blues from having spent some years in a dump.
$35

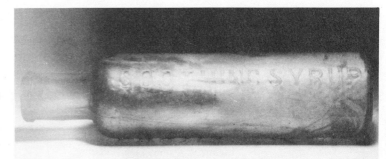

Small blown-in-a-mold pharmacy bottle bought in bulk by the druggist, cork-stoppered.
$35

Twelve-sided apothecary bottle about 4 inches long.
$25

59

Apothecary bottles with brilliant black-and-gold labels reverse-painted on thin pieces of glass that were then glued to the bottles. You could buy bottles blank and then buy the plates you wanted to put on them. Depending on size, **$25–$50** each.

"Lightning" canning jar. Lightning-fast top, goes on fast to speed up Granny's work in the kitchen. Commonly available, but still costs around **$15**; more if interesting colored glass.

Bottle in the shape of the Eiffel Tower, about 10 inches high, that was dated 1937. Could the original have been built in 1837? From France, and originally was filled with French Za-Rex drink syrup. **$35**. Less in France.

60

Bowls

Oval chopping bowl about 14 inches long. Over **$50** in this good shape.

Two round wooden bowls. The cracked one still goes for **$25**; the larger sound one for **$40**. The pestle for **$8**.

Nice figuration on this burl bowl, the rarest of them all. Depending on size, shape, and condition, burl bowls sell for from
$400–$2,000

Turned wood sugar bowl with its original cover and some nice grain painted decoration. So it is a $150 bowl with $400 worth of painted decoration, making it a **$550–$600** bowl. And if you think that no one has ever thought of faking the old grain decoration of these things, you have another think coming. Caveat emptor.

Boxes

German porcelain tobacco boxes from the 1880s with nice animal paintings on them. Very sought after. Each
$125

About 18 inches long, a dome-topped box with nice, solid brasses and leaf-decorated leather outside surface. Could be used to keep deeds and valuable papers in. About
$85

Small steamer trunk that has been stripped down to some nice-looking pine, stained, and oiled.
$60–$75

Dome-topped trunk with pressed metal hinges and handles.
$75

Nice deed box with nail decoration. Leather has been removed because it had gotten ratty.
$45

Lots of character to this 18-inch-long, dome-topped deed box. Fine false graining and other painting make this worth
$150

Advertising trade box for rubber gloves.
$40.

63

Pantry boxes are always quick movers, taking the place of the old Shaker boxes that nobody can find anymore. Pine covers and bottoms, beech or ash sides. **$30–$150** depending on size and whether they are interestingly painted to tell what they held.

Sweet cardboard hatbox from the big city. For the fun of it
    $35

Chiquita banana boxes sell for **$3–$5** apiece. Why? Because they are a collectible that you can carry your other collectibles in. Dealers buy them at flea markets because you can use them over and over.

Tin lithographed bread box.
    $25

64

Wood Kennedy's biscuit box selling for $40 because of the name on the label. Other such boxes
    $15

Beautifully painted and patinaed cover on this common cheese box pushes the price up to $175 for folk art. Folk art is big! The trick is to see it where other people only see a cheese box.

Eight-inch-long trinket box. But factory-stenciled and -painted. No talent, no feeling, no humanity, and therefore no art.
    $15

65

Brass and Bronze Pieces

Ten-inch-rim-diameter solid brass dinner bell inscribed "Property of U.S. Navy." A solid investment at
   $125

Brass/copper coal hod in the helmet style.
   $150

Twelve-inch brass bucket that has seen better days. With wrought-iron rim and missing its bail handle.
   $50

Brass blowtorches catch the eye.
$45–$60

Set of brass weights fitted into wood box. Store item. **$75** for a complete set.

Agate stone with 3-inch-long bronze goose. Mass-produced, but even so, **$125**. Bronze is brown. Brass is yellow. Brass is copper with zinc in it. Bronze is copper with tin in it. Both harden the copper, but bronze is harder than brass. Both are poured into molds.

One-foot-high brass bust on marble base. High shine and high art imported from France. Art Nouveau period.
$1,200

Brass sheet stencils used to label the ends of wood boxes. Each
$25

Another bronze. Jaguar on agate base.
$125

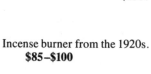

Nine-inch-long brass shark, or maybe it's supposed to be a killer whale. Amateur work. Primitive?
$150?

Incense burner from the 1920s.
$85–$100

Pan and his pipes is white metal with applied paint to look like antique bronze patina. Made in Italy. Sold as a souvenir, but it is a fake to watch out for. Bronze is heavier than white metal —a hardened lead. Still this piece is worth
$65

Incense burner in the Egyptian manner, bronze. Top of roasting pan comes off. Quaint.
$125–$150

Eighteen inches high, this work has a bronze face and a marble cowl. **$850– $1,100**, depending on how much taste and money you have.

Conventional eagle brass door knocker with excellent patina to make it worth **$125–$150**. The shiny new ones are around **$45**.

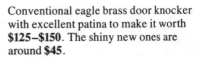

English door knocker.
$125

Single candlestick from Near East with typical embossed pattern.
$40

Handle of fire tongs; polished brass. This one
$25

Brass harness buckle from England.
$40

Six-inch-wide footed bronze jewelry case from India. If you want to buy it as an antique, pay **$200**. If you want to buy it as a fake, **$25**. This one happens to be a fake, but since it is made the same way that the old ones were, although the patina is chemically rushed, there isn't really any way to tell the difference.

70

Reproduction brass andirons shouldn't
go for more than
$125

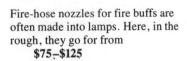

Fire-hose nozzles for fire buffs are
often made into lamps. Here, in the
rough, they go for from
$75-$125

Reproduction brass andirons with
Chippendale bases on them. The pair,
$150-$200

Collection of brass candlesticks; from
$50-$150, depending on size and ornateness of design.

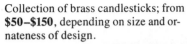

Buttons and Pins

Celluloid portrait button with the flavor
of the late 1800s.
$30

Wasn't Hubert always a wonderful
man!
$15–$20

Batman and Robin go for only
$5

Pewter-looking metal pin that is so funny someone could easily get **$25**. It reads "MAFIA—Mothers And Fathers Italian Association," and it is fifty years old.

Brass buttons from police uniforms command **$5** apiece.

Police badge with eagle on top.
$25

Candy Containers

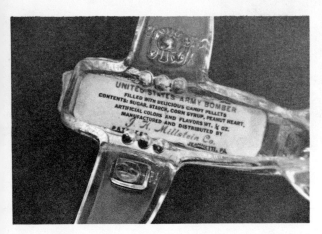

Mostly made in Germany. Candy was held in by a piece of cardboard stuck in the bottom. Originally they sold for 5 cents, but soared in price over the years to 15 cents. Today they run from **$35–$65**. This airplane is a steal at the **$25** price marked on it. Should go for **$45**.

Glass chicken
$65

Sedan
$25

Jeep, cheap,
$15

Nail-polish red wheels.
$40

Battleship with nail-polish red on top of
smokestacks.
$35

Cast Iron

Under 20 inches, a doorstop for the tack-room door.
$75

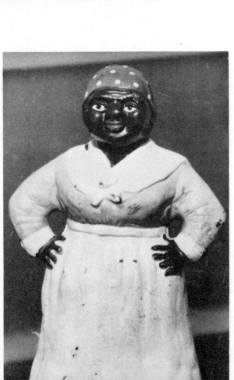

Cast-iron groom hitching post holds a lantern.
$350–$450

Mammy-doll doorstop.
$35

Pair of Hessian soldier andirons, widely reproduced. Reproductions go for **$75**. Authentically old ones for **$450**. Mostly they sell to people whose names end in "tz" and are descended from Hessian soldiers who decided to settle in Pennsylvania and the Hudson Valley when Cornwallis blew it for George III.

Cast-iron cabin doorstop—Uncle Tom's cabin, that is. Rare, art, and "black."
$350

Fancy parlor stove. The more chrome the more money. There is a store full of them on the famous antiques street up in Hallowell, Maine, just outside of Augusta. Fully restored they run from **$500–$1,000**. This one is worth
$750

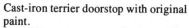

Cast-iron terrier doorstop with original paint.
$65

Victorian inkstand with pair of Baccarat bottles with brass tops on them. Stand is gilded cast iron. Baccarat is best French glass—like Irish crystal.
$110

Child's dollhouse stoves with lids and skillets go for about
$150

Mexican dinner bell, cast iron faked up to look like bronze.
$35

Polychromed child-and-dog cast-iron doorstop.
$85

78

Nice paint job and glass eyes on an owl doorstop of cast iron. Careful paint job, in excellent condition.
$100

Conventional potted flowers, cast-iron doorstop.
$55

Repainted lady bootjack, widely reproduced.
$45

Cast-iron elephant bookends with a fake-bronze applied patina. Very nice. For the pair,
$100

Ceramics

Toothpick holder with ruffled edge is a
copy of a Dresden pattern. Souvenir
novelty. German.
$25–$40

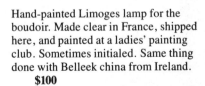

Hand-painted Limoges lamp for the
boudoir. Made clear in France, shipped
here, and painted at a ladies' painting
club. Sometimes initialed. Same thing
done with Belleek china from Ireland.
$100

Mantelpiece cat, early gift shop style.
$20–$40.(Some people just love cats.)

80

Staffordshire dogs usually come in pairs from 8–20 inches tall. Hand-painted at factory. Reddish browns better than blacks. Or greens. Some have glass eyes. This pair
$125

Hand-painted pink lusterware cup and saucer, house-pattern decoration.
$50

Tomatoware marked Royal Bayreuth, very finely made German china. Each
$65–$85

Dinner set made in England by Booth, of no great age but old enough to have some charm. From early 1900s. The complete set
$150–$200

81

Part of an English breakfast set decorated with green foliage. Marked Rockingham. These pieces **$300**

S.E.G. pitcher made by Boston Pottery. Lustrous orange panels, white base, black lines. Early 1900s on. **$45**. Highly underappreciated at this time. This stuff is very arty, very American.

Small spongeware pitcher worth
$25

Copper lusterware pitcher 6 inches high.
$65

82

Chocolate set of Limoges china with blown-bottom pitcher.
$225

Hand-painted blank vase from Germany in the Victorian era.
$55

Hand-painted Limoges china vase. This piece
$85

Small chinaware vase, early gift or souvenir shop. Flowers are an applied transfer. Outline is gold leaf. Cheap-looking but has lots of charm and romance to it. **$35**, and underrated in today's market.

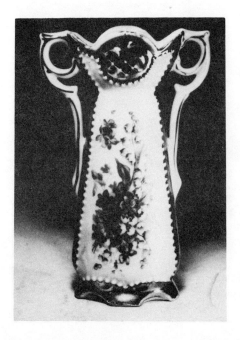

Nicely decorated toothbrush holder
from a pitcher-and-bowl bathroom set.
$25

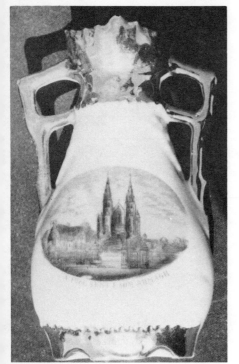

Souvenir vase 6 inches high, gold leaf,
applied transfer picture.
$25–$35

Two-handled vase in English porcelain.
$25

Limoges china, elaborate, 1890–1910,
vine-shaped handles of Art Nouveau
era.
$125–$150

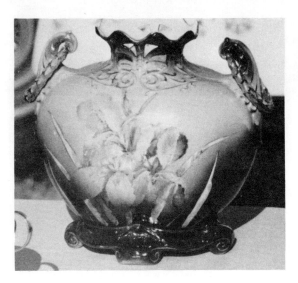

Hand-painted German china vase.
English ones have fancier bottoms.
$55

Eight-inch-high hatpin holder from
1920s.
$35–$50

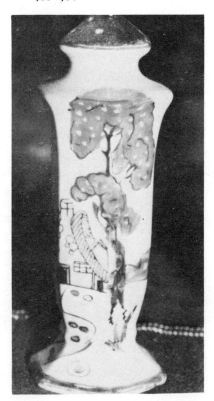

Irish carnival piece with very colorful
applied transfer.
$35

Wedgwood pitcher with twisted handle,
dark-blue color with white inside and
figures.
$85–$125

Washbowl and pitcher in ordinary china with pretty bunch of flowers. Always worth **$85–$125** depending on how perfect the edges are (free of even glaze chipping is perfect) and who is selling it where and to whom.

Gold-banded, plain white pitcher and bowl.
$75–$85

Flow-blue China made for export to the U.S. (from China, of course). Would you believe handleless cups are up to **$60** each. The handled cups, **$35**; the pitcher, **$75**; saucers, **$15**.

Un bol de nuit complete with cover and nice delicate decoration. The tighter the cover fits the better the piece. This one
$65

86

Hand-painted Limoges done anywhere from the 1890s to the 1920s. Done by upper-class women at art classes long before liberation arrived.
$75–$100

Gravy boat of the English persuasion with good applied handles and still has original ladle in it with handle sticking out.
$125–$150

1920s coleslaw pottery, 7 inches tall. Factory product.
$15

Clocks

Pressed-oak gingerbread clock with stenciled glass in bottom. Chimes strike.
$175–$250

Nice brass mantel clock of the French persuasion. Good figure, good clock with separate time and chime springs that run a week. Imported new during early Victorian era.
$250–$300

Oak mantel clock, unusual Grecian-
building style.
$125

Marble Seth Thomas mantel clock with
brass decorations drilled in.
$150–$175

Gilded cast-iron building clock. Grecian idea. Washington, D.C., Lincoln
Memorial building.
$125

Miniature steeple clock with rosewood
veneer case. Even in need of repair,
$125. Fixed, **$175**. Old. Mid-1800s.

89

Imitation marble mantel clock of wood.
Ebonized finish, marble false graining.
$40–$50

Good reverse-painting panel on this
paw-footed split-column shelf clock.
Made by Daniel Pratt of Reading, Massachusetts. Can also be screwed to the
wall. Hepplewhite oval inlay in crest is
weird replacement of original Empire
panel. Nevertheless . . .
$175

"Glass and Brass" clock with enameled
dial. Most made in England for U.S.
trade. A few made in Fair Haven, Ver-
mont. This English one **$300**. Fair
Haven ones worth **$650–$750**. This is
Grecian style of late 1800s.

Grouping of ordinary shelf, cottage, or
kitchen clocks. Depending on condition,
$35–$75

Big Ben by Westclox, the original 8-inch-tall model of the early 1920s. Made by Western Clock Co. in La Salle, Illinois, distributed through local jewelers who got their name imprinted on the face. Every one as good a clock as it was when it was first made, and should last another five hundred years.
$125–$150

Detail photo of controls on Big Ben clock reading "Steady, Repeat, Silent, Alarm."

"Glass and Brass" clock of the early 1900s is French Art Nouveau style. Cheap white-metal castings, though, make it worth less than it looks to be at first glance.
$200–$250

Back of a "Glass and Brass" clock showing visibility of the works. This is a good one that came with two candelabras for **$650** the set.

91

Clothes

Hat from 1920s with cut ribbons and artificial flowers of chiffon. Coming into vogue again.
$25

Victorian evening purse, semiprecious stones, tasseled pulls, much sought after by the denizens of New York City night life right now.
$55–$65

Victorian evening purses with sewn-on beads and semiprecious stones. Each
$50–$75

"Ostrich Tail" bag with very colorful beads on jet background. Britannia Metal clasp.
$150

Original Lincoln-type beaver hat with leather travel case, brass lock. Stiffened felt made of beaver fur, brushed on outside. Brush comes in case.
$150

Clasp from a lady's purse from Art Deco period.
$25

Afternoon hat from the 1920s.
$25–$30

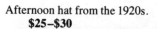

Lady's Panama hat on which you would change the flowers each season.
$25

Antique ladies' hats running from **$20–$40**, and a man's straw hat for only **$10**.

Small lady's sewing purse for use when traveling.
$35

94

A rack of antique dresses that are very popular with the cocktail-party set. This selection runs from **$25–$40**, but many run up to **$200**—the sequined evening gowns, for instance. (In fine condition or restored, of course.)

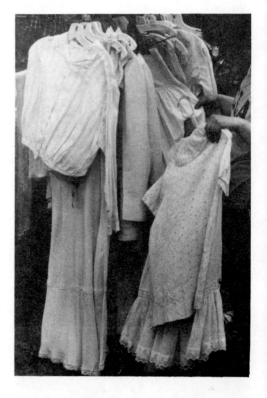

Oh, remember the girls in their summer blouses.
$35–$75

Copper

Coffee urn from a roadside diner of the '20s and '30s. These are chrome-plated copper, and sell for around
$350

Brightly shined copper funnel.
$35

Electroplated baby shoe. There's always *somebody* who will buy *anything*.
$40

Copper kettle with spout dovetailed into body. Handle also. Best kind. Six-quart.
$125

Brass-and-copper fire extinguisher brightens up any room, as they say. Make good floor or table lamps. Your local insurance man's office isn't complete without one. Around
$100

Cups and Saucers

Simple moustache cup.
$25

Shaving mugs—to the left an Odd Fellows one, kept at the local barbershop before Gillette came along. Most had simply the client's last name on them. Occupational ones are better. Named ones range from **$45–$75**. Occupational ones are **$125–$165**.

Right-handled moustache cup with gold lining.
$45

Shaving mug with side pouch for the soap. Souvenir.
$40

German china cup and saucer in the oriental manner.
$40

German china cup and saucer in a Dresden pattern.
$35

Souvenir cup with fine pressed-glass base, so fine it is called "near-cut." Clear red lacquer flashed on top. Usually inscribed in gold leaf. Carnivals.
$35

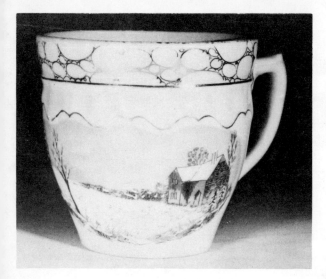

Simple German cup with a house scene
on it from 1890s. Should have a large
saucer with it. The cup alone
$25

Teacup from Germany also missing its
saucer. Souvenir china.
$14

German teacup *with* its saucer goes for
$35

Decoys

Folk art, sort of, duck decoy.
$75–$100

Very graceful goose decoy.
$125–$150

Nice paint, glass eyes, wire legs pin-tail shorebird. Actually a wood carving for your study, not a working decoy. **$250**. (If it was an original Crowel one, **$3,500**.)

Ugly pair of primitive decoys. The pair,
$125

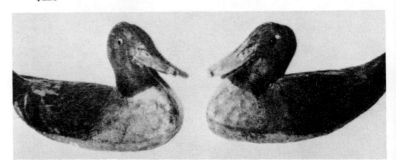

Grouping of assorted-neck goose decoys, handmade, not very old, but very
good. **$75–$100**. Lots coming out of
Canada these days. (Actually antique
ones in the **$500–$700** range.)

Nicely painted back on this duck decoy.
Contemporary artist.
$125

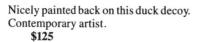

Nicely weathered piece of folk art.
$125

Dolls

Palmer-Cox Brownie doll with bug eyes. Early 1900s policeman. Six inches high.
$225

Black-faced corn-husk doll from Maryland.
$25

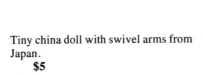

Tiny china doll with swivel arms from Japan.
$5

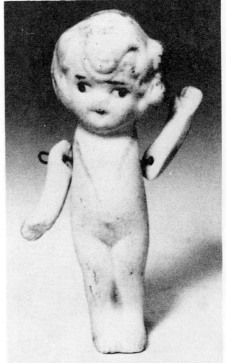

103

Composition head, garden-variety doll.
$25

Best of its class. Burlap doll that looks
like a drunken monkey. **$35**. I wish I'd
bought the old rascal.

Black stocking doll.
$30

Parian-head doll with open mouth and
sleeping eyes. French origin. Circa
$250

China-head doll with molded hair, padded body. French origin.
$125

Bisque-head doll with glass eyes, open mouth, real hair, and straw hat. Nicely hand-painted.
$300–$350

Crude Parian-head doll with molded head that includes bonnet. Typical padded body.
$65

Tiny celluloid doll in baby dress.
$35

Bisque Japanese Kewpie doll.
$40

Bisque Kewpie-style baby for piano top.
$45

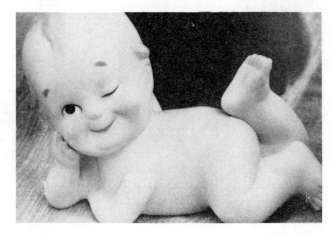

China-head doll with glass eyes, closed mouth, and real hair wig.
$150

Group of collectible dolls, mostly Parians, which can range anywhere from **$150–$500**

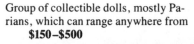

Interestingly painted eyes on this French bisque doll with long real human hair.
$175–$200

106

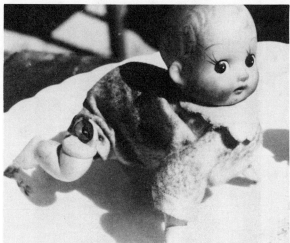

Wind-up creeping doll of celluloid with
stationary painted eyes.
$55

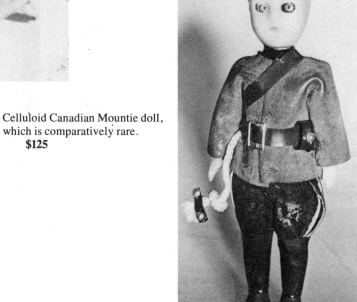

Celluloid Canadian Mountie doll,
which is comparatively rare.
$125

Papier-mâché head with kidskin body.
In the range of
$125

Hand-sewn rag doll with yarn hair.
$60

Tiny all-molded bisque dolls. About
$15

Souvenir trade doll from Alaska. Baby
seal skin.
$75

Stuffed fabric Babe Ruth doll.
$75

Celluloid 4-inch-high Babe Ruth doll
made in Japan.
$85

Irish Paddy doll in shiny bisque.
$25

Life-sized Shirley Temple composition doll.
$650

Papier-mâché molded-head doll that needs to be touched up.
$45

Schoenhut clown doll from Germany with carved and hand-painted wood head.
$125

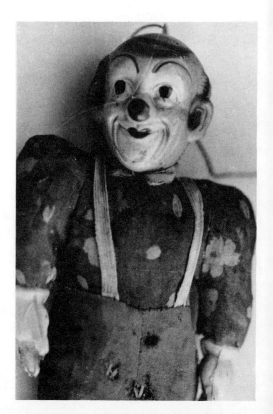

Farm and House

Old postcard showing seed salesman calling on a couple of New York State farmers all dressed up for the photograph. Seeds were sold by showing hand-colored lithographs of the final result as in following two photographs.

Close-up of print for the "Kelsey Japan Plum." Brilliantly hand-colored. Framed, each sells for from
$45–$75

Close-up of a book of hand-colored seed prints just like the one shown on salesman's lap in postcard photo. Thirty prints in the book. At only **$30** per unframed print, the book is an easy
$900

Ox yoke, now selling for from **$85–$125** in New England. Easily double that in Texas.

Very antique salt box with little drawer for matches.
$200 plus

Coffee grinder made into a lamp.
$55

Well-photographed kid's wheelbarrow, high-Victorian. Burned-in squirrel decoration.
$125

Pierced tin foot warmer to go under the blankets when you are out in your horse and buggy on a cold winter's night. Tin-bowl inside of it holds hot coals.
$125

Wall-mounted coffee mills with measuring cup.
$35–$45

Hand eggbeater of cast iron.
$30

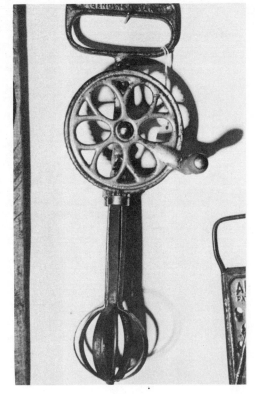

Cherry-pitter that attaches to the table? French toleware cheese grinder? Either way,
$35

112

Small 5″ x 8″ stormway mirror to check yourself out before going out into a New England winter. Veneered Empire frame. An honest-to-God antique.
$75

Butter stamps used to tell what month or season the butter was made.
$35–$150

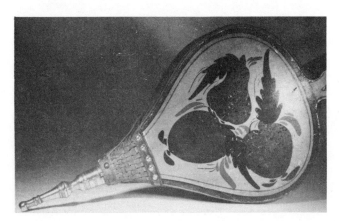

Hand-decorated turtleback bellows with brass nozzle. Commonly reproduced or faked—i.e., new decoration. But this is real, so
$165

Four-inch-long bellows used to dry your ink.
$15

113

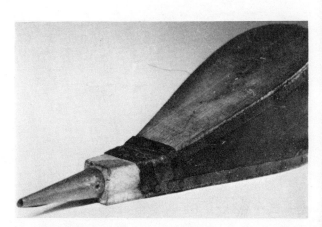

Child-size shoe stretcher, adjustable.
$12

Very rare butter paddle with stamp on handle, 10 inches long. How rare? **$500** worth rare.

Cleaned-up coffee mills. The brass one on right is better.
$45 and **$65**

Unopened box of the original Gold Dust twins soap powder.
$2

114

Five inches wide and made of soft, bendable lead, these three dogs toasting the king are a veddy British joke beyond explanation. Souvenir piece.
$65

Ornamental statue 10 inches high from the Victorian era made of marble dust and cast in a mold. Shiny surface washes off and sharpness dissolves when washed with soap and water. Don't wash yours unless you want it to get the ancient Greek look this washed one has. Mint **$65**. This washed one **$25**.

Victorian candlestick of china, with brown glaze.
$20

Ten-inch-tall mantelpiece ornament.
German, hand-painted china.
$40

Late-1920s imitation Dresden figure 10
inches tall.
$50

Top of a pillow doll with
real hair and net.
$25

Bride and groom for top of a wedding
cake in the 1930s.
$15–$25

Hummel boy.
$125

Carved wood figure, 12 inches high, from a birth-of-Christ scene. One of the three kings. European origin.
$65

1920s plaster cast of a monkey sitting on book labeled "Darwin" as he contemplates a human skull. **$45**. Now I've seen everything.

Ginger beer stoneware jugs hand-painted winter scenes. The pair,
$350

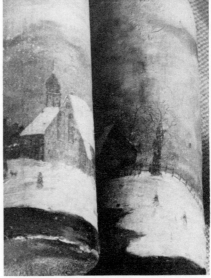

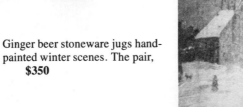

117

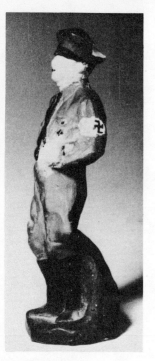

Plaster of paris, 6-inch-high figure of Adolf Hitler. Brought home by a veteran of World War II. **$65** for the horror of it.

General Douglas MacArthur looking like a boy. Twelve inches high, composition.
$50

Maggie and Jiggs. Plaster of paris carnival prizes, about 7 inches high.
$40

Bronze finish on plaster of paris.
$25

Does anybody know what this is, so we can tell in the next edition? Seems to be solid bronze, but what organization does it represent? An eye is in man's chest. Letters on shield are "SYKO." The dealer who owns it has been trying to find out about it for fifteen years. Not for sale.

Two-inch-high family mascot. Boy blowing flute. German china.
$15

Figure for railroad train set looking for all the world like George Grosz's burghers.
$15

His wife.
$15

Folk Art

Hand-painted Belleek mug about the
"Irish Problem."
$125

Wood circus figure, probably a leopard,
5 inches long.
$60

Wedge of wood painted in shape of a
watermelon. It's really very old. The
new ones are $6.50.
$125

Decorative wood carving, 3 feet high and 7 feet long, recently done on the coast of Maine.
$1,400

Hand-carved wood eagle in the landing position, 18 inches high.
$350

Old trade sign 2 feet wide.
$200

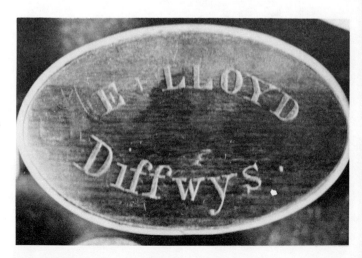

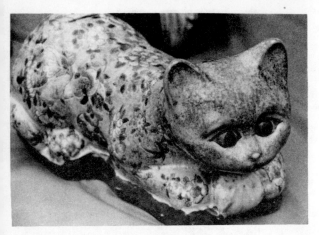

Fired polychromed pottery cat. Very colorful.
$75

Giant pig over 3 feet long. Recent carving. Burgundy red, glazed.
$650

Ten-inch-high wood statuette used in Catholic churches under the Spanish influence.
$65

Finely carved head from a santo figure originally found in a Spanish Catholic mission in New Mexico.
$250

Incised stoneware, blue decoration on
gray body, 12 inches high.
$125

Seed box with advertising label in
super-good condition. It has been filled
with hand-carved reproductions of watermelon, asparagus, carrots, etc.
$350

Imitation ship's figurehead carved on a
Pacific Ocean island.
$400

Hand-painted chicks on a barmaid's
wine cask; carried on her wrist.
$350

Saki bottle, 10 inches tall, pale blue.
$75

Painted jewel box in the early Pennsylvania manner. A real antique.
$175

Canadian carving, about 4 feet tall, of a
knight.
$250

Homemade of wood and pieces of tin—
with about a 2-foot wingspread—this is
really folk art. At least
$225

124

Life-size knight from ancient France.
Worm-eaten wood with gesso surface.
$550–$650

Hand-decorated German teapot.
$125

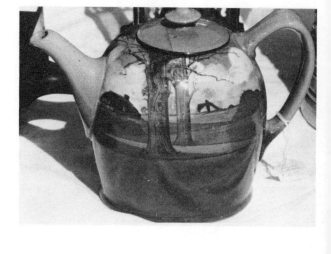

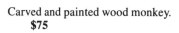

Hand-carved model of a shorebird.
$35

Carved and painted wood monkey.
$75

Carved wood monk figure holding a
weird-size baby or child. From south-
western U.S. Chapel figure—not a
santo.
$150

Mexican carving of rooster.
$125

On the left a reproduction of an ancient frame imported from Spain—**$15**. On the right an Art Nouveau period dark silver finish on gesso on wood frame, 5″ x 8″
   $35

Brass-finished tin oval on velvet panel. Antique, Spanish.
   $35

Group of Victorian walnut frames: **$15** for the square ones, **$20** for the oval ones.

127

Standard Victorian walnut frame 12 inches high, with gold-leafed liner.
$18

Nice color print of Pope John.
$15

Cast-iron and gilded French Victorian Art Nouveau frame, 12 inches high.
$85

Victorian cast-iron and gilded frame with cupids.
$125

Gold-leafed oval frame 18 inches tall. Brand-new import from Europe, but looks old.
$16

Victorian shaving mirror of gilt-dipped tin.
$45

Group of frames from the 1920s and '30s; **$5–$20** for the one in the middle.

Very sought-after Art Nouveau picture frame, cast iron, bronze-plated (often called "dipped"). In the **$150–$175** class.

Tabletop pool table, 3 feet long. Victorian parlor pool. Complete and in nice condition.
$250

The classic, full-grown, one-armed bandit with no nonsense about gum balls—just "give me your money or your life." Fully restored and the works rebuilt to last a thousand years.
$1,800–$2,200

Counter-top gum-ball machine, one-armed bandit about 18 inches high.
$650

Variation on the "three cherries" game, this one plays five-card poker. But everybody still wants the three cherries, so this one is only
$350

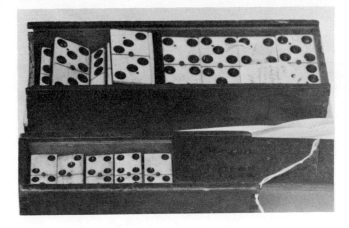

Ivory dominoes were made on whaling boats just like scrimshaw was. Hollowed-out dots painted black with a mixture of soot and shellac. Partial set **$125**. Complete set **$250**.

German toy licensed to be made in Philadelphia.
$75

Victorian lawn croquet set. In original box. I wish I'd bought these, too.
$65–$75

Parlor table racehorse roulette for the racier Victorian home.
$350–$400

131

Anything to do with Popeye cuts the mustard. Even cardboard. You try to throw the rings onto his pipe stuck in the mouth of the cardboard figure.
$48

Early Parker Brothers game made in Salem, Massachusetts. All are valuable. Johnny's Historical is worth **$125** any day.

Very early Parker Brothers game gives Salem, Massachusetts, as its only address. Later ones, such as the Indians game, also give New York and London. This game
$125

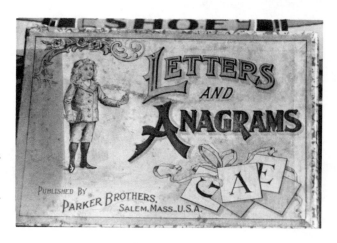

Another Parker Brothers game.
$75–$100

132

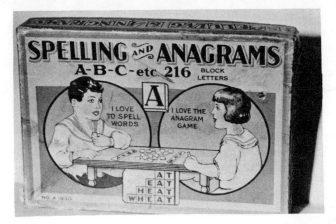

Spelling and Anagrams set of blocks.
$60

Carnival wheel. Where it stops nobody
knows. Wheel of fortune or vertical
roulette.
$150

Group of checkerboards, **$150–$300**,
depending on how attractive the colors
and patina are.

Héns and Geese, a really early American antique. Museum quality.
$250

133

Glass

Signed art glass in the **$200–$250** class. A bowl to put rose petals in.

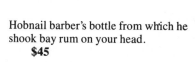

Hobnail barber's bottle from which he shook bay rum on your head.
$45

Square inkstand that originally came from a lap desk. Square to fit in partitions. Leakproof cap.
$25

Pressed-glass many-faceted inkstand.
$35

Product of Pierpoint Glass Co.
Pewter-caped inkstand.
$55

Hat-shaped inkwell that was stoppered
with a cork.
$55

Glass paperweight, gold-sprayed. With
the paint taken off,
$20

Multicolored fruit-design free-blown
paperweight.
$120

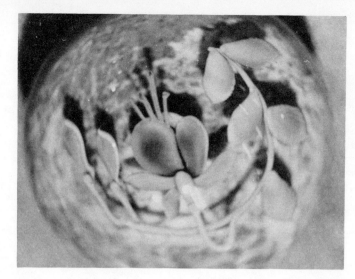

Run-of-the-míll blue telephone-pole
glass insulator.
$15

Lalique, fancy French glass bowl.
$450–$500

Lalique clock holder from a French
dresser set.
$125–$150

136

Famous "Daisey & Button" pressed-glass pattern on a top-hat toothpick holder. Window piece.
$45

Milk-glass top-hat toothpick holder, hand-painted in Germany.
$25

Pair of art-glass vases with applied colored fruit on the sides. Milk-glass base with clear-glass ruffles on top. Rough pontils, showing they are hand-blown. Six or 7 inches high.
$145

Nailsea pattern art-glass vase worth
$50–$70

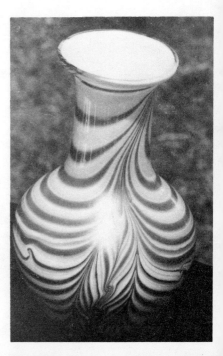

Guns

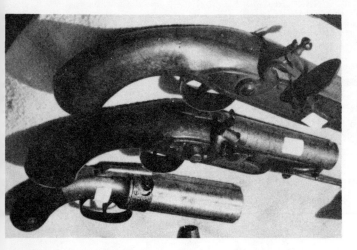

Grouping of two percussion pistols and a flintlock. The pepperbox style in the foreground, **$300**; middle one with ramrod under barrel, **$250**; the flintlock on top, **$250–$400**.

Smallest of the above is a lady's boot gun, **$65**. Frontier Colt on top, **$265**. Flintlock pistol in middle, **$375**. Gambler's Colt on the bottom, **$250**.

Percussion-cap guns on each side run from **$150–$225**. The flintlock in the middle, **$350–$550**.

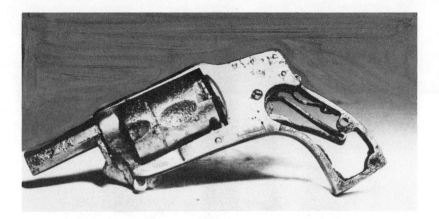

Snub-nose revolver carried in the
Spanish Civil War.
$25

Brass cannon 6 inches long on cast-iron
carriage.
$150–$200

Polychromed terra-cotta piece for an
entry-hall plant stand. An original, old
piece.
$550–$650

Soft-sculpture elephant about 18 inches
high, decorated with sewn-in mirrors,
etc. Recently made, but better than an
antique one because the old ones have
all fallen apart.
$150

Ornately carved wooden horse about 3 feet high. Recent duplication of an ancient palace decoration.
$350

Reproduction of historical decorative figure in hollow-cast bronze. Very religious people. Three feet high.
$275

There isn't too much I want to say about this baked terra-cotta frieze decoration from an Indian temple, except that it is 15 inches tall and if stolen and smuggled into the U.S. it is worth **$1,500**. If it is a reproduction made the same way as an original, **$350**.

141

Jewelry

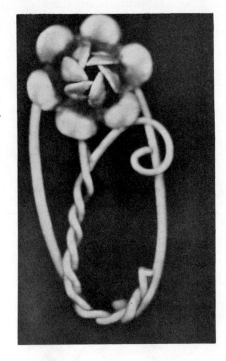

Twisted silver-wire pin of the arts-and-crafts period.
$35

Real cultured pearls on this gold-filled brooch bring it to
$45

Art Nouveau meets Grecian in this fine glass-jeweled cameo in gold-filled frame.
$85

Standard cameo set in ten-karat gold frame. Carved out of two layers of stone.
$85

Painted Limoges tile set in gold-filled frame. Hand-painted by arts and crafts ladies, circa 1900.
$35

Fourteen-karat gold watch fob in shape
of basket with seed pearls.
$165

Silver articulated pin 2 inches wide.
$45

Silver-dipped white-metal pin with
glass diamonds and plastic ruby from
the '20s.
$30

144

Persian pierced-brass table lamp, recently imported. Electrified.
$65

Christmas tree bulb, made in Japan. Strong on nostalgia, it sells for
$35

Pair of carriage lamps from a buggy. The pair,
$175

Not a Tiffany, but a Victorian leaded-glass shade on a white-metal base. About
$750

Finely made reproductions of Tiffany lamps, made the same way as the originals, sell for from **$400–$1,000** each, depending mainly on size. These are real glass and lead—not the cheap plastic ones, which sell for around **$45**.

Close-up of Tiffany reproduction shade worth **$600**. If real, worth **$15,000**. Honest.

Pair of bedroom lamps with alabaster urns and spatter-glass globes. Made by dropping crumbled pieces of different colors of glass into a milky base of molten glass. The pair,
$25

146

Hanging lampshade of milk glass, professionally painted very fast in the factory. Depending on size and condition,
$65–$100

Bristol-glass shade for Rayo or
student-type lamp. **$60** with the chip.
$120 if perfect.

German-made lamp with hand-painted
font, cast-iron base and top, brass-
dipped.
$35

Rayo lamp, originally nickel-plated over brass. Now people remove the nickel to reveal the brass. Milk-glass shade.
$85–$150

Pair of wall-bracket kerosene lamps. Brackets screwed onto wall. Lamps were portable, flat-bottomed, of course. Pair,
$175

Kerosene-burning lamps not yet converted to electricity. Center one with tall glass is from a railroad car; the others often found in public buildings as well as homes.
$75–$150

148

Farm or barn lantern, polished up. Originally sold in the general store for less than $1—now **$25–$40** for a well-polished Dietz (brand name).

Wonderfully rakish country-store lamp that hung from ceiling; could be pulled down for lighting, filling, etc. Made for public buildings, not home use. Depending on quality and condition, **$150–$300**

English-made kerosene lamp with painted font of the usual cottage in the country. Bristol glass holds the kerosene. **$140**

Victorian wall sconce of cast brass with beveled glass in the center. Nice Queen Anne flavor to the design, about 18 inches high, holds two candles. Most likely made in England, but not so marked.
$175–$225

Supposed to be Mickey and Minnie Mouse, these Christmas tree bulbs were (badly) made in Japan, but because of the subject, **$30** each.

150

Military

Memorial plaque from World War I into which you could insert your own photo.
$35

Air raid warden's helmet.
$15

German spiked helmet from World War I, with neck and face guards.
$45

Typical "keep a tight lip" lithographed poster used in wartime England, World War I.
$75

Poster put out by an English labor union *after* World War I. Fine color and artwork. Very interesting subject for history professors. Rare.
$200–$225

Doughboy hats.
$5

Doughboy helmet.
$20

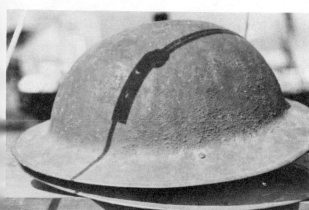

Military Miniatures

Cardboard soldiers set in wooden bases, colored lithography, about 4 inches high. Fifteen in a set, in the original box, are worth
$45

World War I lead soldiers came about seventy-five to a box for $5. Now each soldier sells for about
$4

Composition set of German World War I soldiers. For the boxful,
$25

153

Box of English lead soldiers, not in
original box. Come in sets of twenty-
four or forty-eight. English mark on
base. Pliable lead so rifles can be bent
back into shape. Colorfully hand-
painted on an assembly line. The set of
twenty-four,
$175

Detail of lead soldier from English set.

Lead sailor, even in this shape, is worth
$2. Repainting them is fun for some
people, and this one would then be
worth **$5**

From World War I, these objects are
American-made of lead and have cast-
iron wheels. Make nice presents for re-
tired military people. Per article,
$25–$40

154

Finely done English-made lead soldiers
like this go for **$45** per piece.

American-made Civil War lead soldiers
with nice detail are worth about **$10**
each. Cheap.

Working sunset cannon. Note touch-
hole on top of back end of brass barrel.
Cast-iron carriage.
    $45

Miniatures

Pair of miniatures painted on ivory, about 1½ inches high. Done from 1790s to 1860s, mostly in Europe as the style of these two indicates. For this pair, **$600**

Costume indicates this to be an American miniature from about 1860. Here shown life size.
$300

American miniature, circa 1880, not as finely done as the English ones, as can be seen in this twice-life-size photo.
$175

English miniature shown twice life size. Done on ivory in the manner of Sir Joshua Reynolds—costume and pose anyway. Gold-filled oval frame.
$500

English miniature blown up *four* times life size to show incredible detail with which these things were done.

American miniature, circa 1820.
$160

Typical English miniature painting on ivory—1860s.
$250

157

Miscellaneous

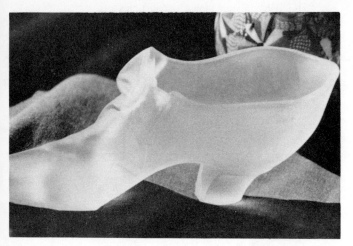

Camphor-glass shoe, 6 inches long.
$50

German portrait plate signed by artist.
Titian hair, fine border.
$125–$150

Japanese Nippon tea set from the 1920s.
Orange luster, cheap china, but worth
$85 and a "comer."

S.E.G. pottery from Boston Pottery. Time of Tiffany, off-yellow background, orange and strong blue with black lines. Hand-done at the pottery. **$65–$100** and another "comer."

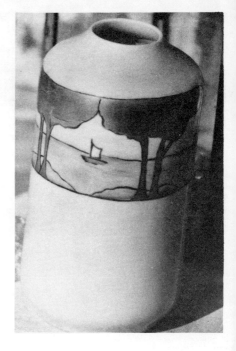

German mantel vases. Portraits are applied transfers in imitation of hand-painted ones. Richly cheap look of charm to some people of great sophistication like me. The pair worth
$88–$100

German cheese dish, with delicate decoration and a leafage handle on it to make it worth
$65

Canoe-shaped pickle boat. Souvenir type of thing, but very nicely done. Seven inches long.
$65

Souvenir houseplant waterer, 6 inches high.
$25–$30

China bird on a treetop. Stands out, but not particularly delicate.
$25

Limoges-type bowl lacking the delicacy of the real thing. For floating heads of flowers in. Hand-decorated. **$50–$75**

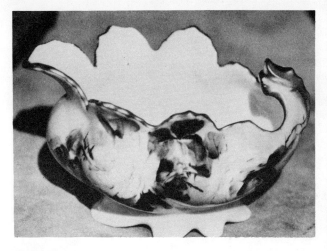

Toby jugs. English Dalton china. Souvenir jugs from London. **$35–$75**, depending on size.

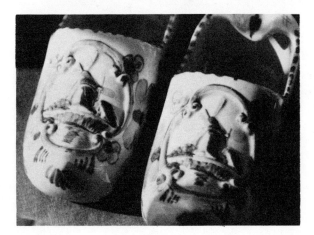

Pair of light-blue Delft chinaware boots. Good to keep matches in over the fireplace.
$35

Gold-flashed and green leaf design bonbon dish.
$25

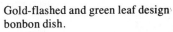

Toothpick holder showing applied black line transfer of Custom House in Bath, Maine. Souvenir. Sold by the local jeweler. **$25–$50**, depending on scarcity.

Crude imitation of Royal Bayreuth tomatoware. For catchup, in a boardinghouse.
$15

Fulper pottery frog that looks like green-patinaed bronze. Goes inside vase or deep dish to hold flower stems. Signed piece. Well worth
$250

162

Molds

Tin mold for making chocolate sitting ducks.
   $40

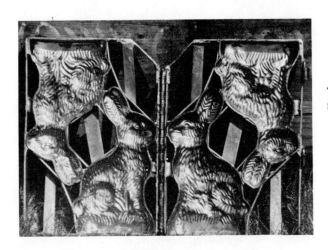

Tin Easter chocolate mold, open, to make two bunnies at once.
   $85

Cast-iron framework keeps a tight fit so the chocolate doesn't leak out.
   $45

Unusual cowboy mold with spring clips on the left and top. But small and modern.
$20

Kickapoo Indian medicine. Because it is funnier than most others,
$15

Musical

Mandolin from the 1920s.
$75

Saxophone from the '30s, in good condition.
$40

Concertina in its original box, **$75**.
Fancier ones go for a lot higher.

Toy drum, on top, of some age and wear, **$12**. Marching band drum, on bottom, with eagle,
$40

Autoharps go very low.
$15

Table music or Bible stand in cut brass.
$115

Cast-iron base on this dictionary, Bible, or music stand. School furniture.
$15

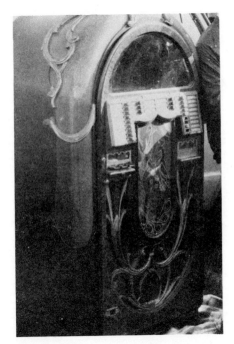

Jukebox from way back in Art Nouveau-Deco period.
$3,500

Sheet music covers are very frameable and sell for from **$5–$10** depending on subject.

167

It's a hand-painted porcelain dial on this brass-cased aeronoid barometer that is 7 inches in diameter.
$75

Antique pocket-size aeronoid barometer, made in England. With brass case,
$175

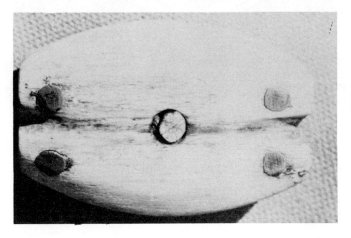

Hand-carved pulley of bone with brass ferrules. Whaling era.
$55

Collection of early seagoing spyglasses with brass caps to go over both lenses. These run
$150–$250

Fine brass seagoing telescope in its case. Case pushes price up to **$350**, more or less.

Ships' pulleys, running here from
$15–$45

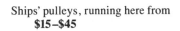

The whole thing! Ship's wheel with binnacle on top of it for your boardroom or president's office. Laminated wheel with brass ferrules is extra touch. **$1,100–$1,250** at Brimfield. The interior decorator gets $3,500 for it.

Round lantern that opens from the top —for lighting on a windy deck, of course.
$85

Brass porthole from a 1920s yacht to hang right on your game-room wall. **$125–$175**, depending on size.

Ships' pulleys have a way of ending up as bases for lamps. This one, with a drum shade, makes **$125** anywhere.

Seven-jewel ship's bell clock. **$125**

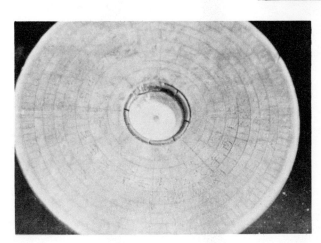

Antique hand-carved wood Chinese compass disc with needle inset. Seven inches wide. **$175**. I should have bought it.

Brass captain's bell. **$150–$250**

171

Beautifully molded brass case of this ship's lantern drives the price up to **$200**

Eighteen-inch-high ship's running light. Port red; starboard green. Polished brass. **$225**

Electrically operated, very loud signal horn. A super-blaster at **$135**

Cased gimbal compass (two swivels, to stay always level) will move smoothly at
$145

Small shiny brass binnacle with small kerosene lamps mounted on either side so you can find it in a hurry and also to light up the compass card inside.
$450

Sextant in its mahogany case out of Liverpool, England, belongs on every library table.
$275

173

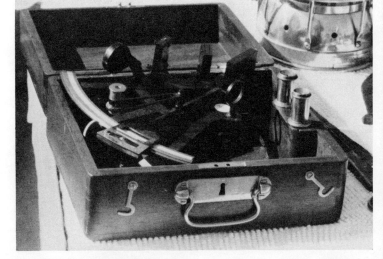

Brass sextant.
$500

A remarkable "whimsy." That is, something a sailor did aboard ship to pass the
time if he was diffident about doing
scrimshaw. This bottle contains an an-
chor, ladder, and assorted tools that
were assembled inside of it.
$125

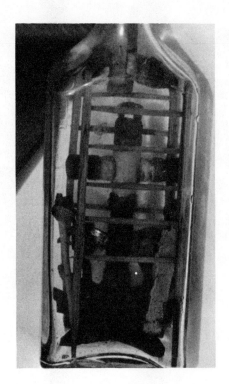

174

Tin lithographed German tray. Lovely scene, 10 inches long. Victorian.
$45

Cloisonné covered jar of no great intricacy of design. Three inches in diameter, factory product.
$20

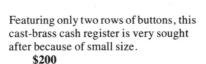

Featuring only two rows of buttons, this cast-brass cash register is very sought after because of small size.
$200

175

Rare portable typewriter that goes for **$35** at a flea market, double that, at least, in a city.

Multiplex typewriter very undervalued by some New England hicks where they sell for around **$18**. City folks, in the advertising game particularly, will go up to **$85** or **$100** for any odd-shaped old typewriter.

Desirable small apothecary chest with glass pulls and reverse painting on glass labels in black, white, and gold leaf; mahogany wood.
$110–$150

Early gum-ball machine with cast-iron base and top, ball glass, **$125**. Square glass ones are later and go for around **$45**.

Fishbowl globe gum-ball machine, hard to find.
$125

Chewing-gum machine.
$75

Store-model coffee grinder with little American eagle finial. Cast iron, old red-and-brass paint, **$250–$300**. This is middle-sized. The larger ones are **$400**; giants, **$500**.

Universal coffee grinder, home kitchen size.
$125

Country store scale in cast iron with brass paint, circa 1915.
$75–$100

178

Unopened bar of pre-Ivory soap.
$2

Unopened bar of soap, **$3** for this one.

Tin deed box ready for stripping and redecoration.
$10

179

Very colorful tin with fine lithographed artwork.
$25

Close-up of pre-Alka-Seltzer tin.

Unopened bar of soap.
$2

Bottle of patent medicine with wonderful copy on label. Gives directions in ten languages for use either "Internally" or "Externally." "Not over 48% alcohol." Sells for
$6

Box that once contained hairnet to use in an open touring car. Cardboard.
$6

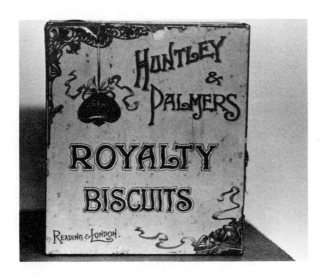

Finely made English tin biscuit box.
$10

Late Victorian tin ice-water dispenser with pewter spigot. Usually found in restaurants.
$65

Old wood-mounted engravings from the days of the flatbed press. Now each about
$3–$7

Marble parrot bookends. Crudely done. The pair,
$30

Souvenir print of the Flatiron Building where the saying "23 skiddoo" originated. It was and still is at Twenty-third Street and Broadway in New York City. Ten inches high. In a thin pressed-brass frame.
$25

Eighteen inches square, the top of a Corinthian column that was once on some public building. Acanthus leaves. Thin lead sheets pressed over wood and plaster. Of interest to interior decorators and architects.
$125

These powder horns run from **$20** for the plain one to **$85** for the one with scratched-in decorations. For dates of battles and portraits, if historic personages owned them, they can go into the thousands of dollars.

Eight inches high, Gothic-shaped portable communion box.
$75

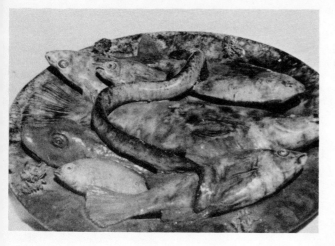

Majolica-style pottery of a plate full of seafood. Twelve inches across.
$85

Framed silhouette portrait, hollow cut, American antique.
$75

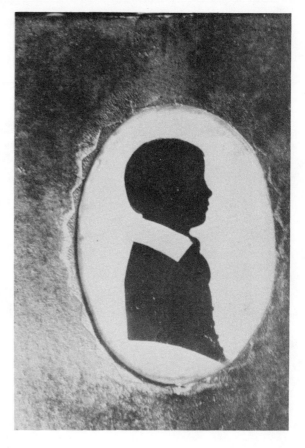

Tin bathtub with wood graining on outside—Victorian.
$125

184

Early beauty-shop mannequin head.
$35

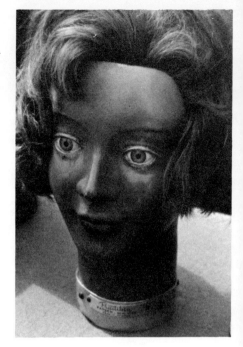

Outside of family photographic album of Victorian era. Pressed brass on red velvet, 14 inches high.
$150

Delegate and organization badges run **$35–$45** for run-of-the-mill conventions. Some special-event badges command three times that.

185

Variety of pocketknives ranging from
$5–$40

Run-of-the-mill brass keys command
only **$1** each. Heavy and ornate ones
run up to **$5**.

Hand-carved antique pillbox.
$25

186

Old enamelware license plates. Depending on the number, they sell for from **$10–$30** each. Lower numbers cost more.

Turtle spittoon in pressed-brass sheet. Step on the head, and the back lifts up to reveal removable glass bowl.
$125

Four-inch-high souvenir of your 1920s visit to the Eiffel Tower.
$15

Victorian doorbell of cast brass is really loud.
$100–$150

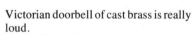

187

Horse-worn sleigh bells are very sought after by interior decorators, going for **$150–$200** a string.

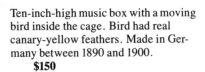

Ten-inch-high music box with a moving bird inside the cage. Bird had real canary-yellow feathers. Made in Germany between 1890 and 1900.
$150

Pottery dancing bear stein.
$45

188

Chinese mask of pottery in the usual
Chinese red and black. Twenties wall
hanging.
$35

Bright red fireman's helmet of gal-
vanized tin. Banged up like this one,
$35. Good ones of this kind, up to **$75**.

Roly-poly tobacco tin about 8 inches
high. Mayo Company put these out in
five different characters. Now, depending upon the paint, up to **$450**, and still
climbing.

This 1920 globe, 20 inches in diameter,
iron frame, and three-legged base of
cast iron, came from a classroom.
Interesting to politically orientated
people.
$80

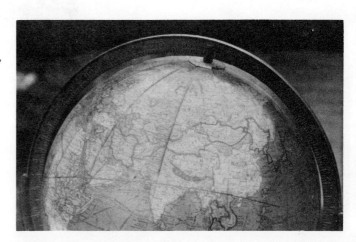

Animal skulls. Foxes, dogs, and monkeys—half human size. Each **$25–$35**

Carved wooden portrait, 2½ feet high, from the outside of the top of a carrousel. Very colorful paint. **$500–$600**

Type trays. Depending on size and richness of color and patina, **$12–$40**

Bone-handle eating utensils with silver-plated wrought-iron blades that really hold a sharp edge. Each **$5–$6**

Eagle Junior safety razor to compete with the Gillette version. **$12**

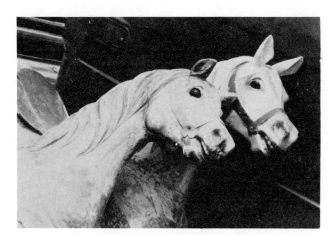

Brightly painted (original) carved wooden carrousel horses. The best ones have the glass eyes and teeth showing like these, and are worth around **$750** each.

Antique bricks with names of their manufacturer on them are worth **$7–$10** each.

Optical

Fine brass transit or "line compass"
worth
  $650

Venerable motion-picture projector. A
penthouse decorative piece going for
$650 in working order.

A good Victorian stereopticon with
which you looked at slides for a third-
dimension effect.
  $70

Magic lantern with flue pipe to carry away fumes of burning kerosene. Good brass lens makes this one worth **$150**. The slides run from **$5–$20** depending on detail and subject matter.

Victorian parlor projector that uses thin glass slides. Generally called a magic lantern. Without slides,
$65

Yale brand magic lantern.
$75–$100

Military field glasses in leather case.
$30

Antique professional microscope in
heavy brass.
$650

Lady's opera glasses with applied
mother-of-pearl. With case,
$50

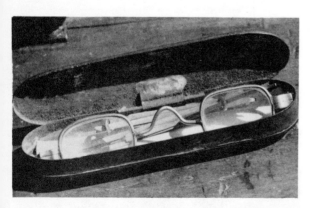

Half-glasses in tin travel case. 1870s.
Gold-washed wire frames.
$22

194

Four inches wide and finely embroi-
dered with gold thread, this slipper be-
longed to a Chinese princess whose feet
had been bound to prevent them from
growing to normal size.
$125

Oriental pottery figure, 12 inches high,
with a mysterious story.
$65

Japanese lacquered brush and crumb tray for keeping your tablecloth looking nice after eating cookies.
$35

Twelve-inch-high vase with lizard handle.
$125

Carved soapstone vase with monkeys from around 1925. Made for export to U.S. from China. Crudely done.
$15

Soapstone carving, 6 inches wide.
$30

196

Japanese pottery made for export, but nicely done. Six inches wide.
$50

Happy Buddha is in shiny glazed pottery, 14 inches high. Recently made, but good.
$125

Eight-inch-high terra-cotta figure.
$30

Pottery horse 6 inches high. Old Chinese-made reproduction in rich deep salmon color.
$65

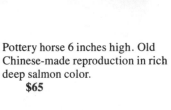

197

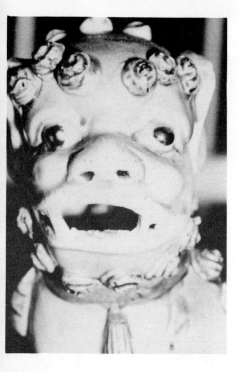

Close-up of a 14-inch-high Fu dog made in China for export. If a recent one, **$20**. If it came in during the '20s, **$110**. Older ones are not stamped "China" on the bottom. However, caveat emptor, since bottoms are sometimes ground off. Also, older ones have more "popped" eyes.

Japanese china that came in between the two world wars and then sold in gift shoppes quite cheaply, but now appreciated enough to go for **$25** for the salt and pepper shakers, **$25** for the creamer, and **$30** for the sugar bowl.

Satsuma-type vase telling a story of Japanese war long past. The 1920s period of oriental imports. Eighteen inches high.
  $75

Paintings

A famous print of the late-Victorian era
—circa 1910. Came in various sizes,
any of which run about
$65

Basically a European Victorian painting done on mahogany board. But it
was found in a New England seaport
town where the whaling ship had obviously been painted in, probably around
1840. Mostly for the oddity of it all,
$250

Oil painting of a transitional coastal steamer.
$600

European pastoral scene.
$175

American impressionism by a student.
$175

"Commercial art" illustration for an early *Collier's* story. On board. For the nostalgia, not the art,
$75

Terrible English reverse painting on glass from Victorian period. Such horrors are ridiculously overvalued at **$75**. Except for the frame, they would be overvalued at 25¢.

From the 1920s this talent-free oil painting on a 15-inch-wide board has a "period" value of **$125** to some people. Elbert Hubbard-type people.

201

Pastel study on a 16″ x 20″ board of
some peaches coming out of a basket.
"Period" value of from
  $40–$65

Fine old oil painting from the late
1800s, but a copy of a famous painting
done earlier of a sea battle in the War of
1812. This copy worth
  $600

Student artists were forever copying
this *Madonna and Child* in Victorian
era. This copy worth
  $350

202

Ancestor portraits, such as this owner of several ships from New Bedford, Massachusetts, sell for from
$800–$900

Grandma Moses may not live again in this 8-inch-square painting on glass, but both sides of the glass are naively attractive. About seventy-five years old, true folk art.
$250

Detail from a collage of artists' signatures in an oil-on-canvas abstraction. Most famous is the signature of Georgia O'Keeffe shown here. Yours for
$125

Pewter

Pewter beaker about 4 inches high. Marked "O Trask"—Oliver Trask from Beverly, Massachusetts. In the **$200** range. Unmarked ones are not antique and go for from **$25–$40**.

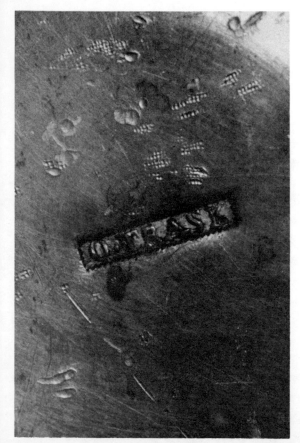

Marking on bottom of pewter beaker.

204

Two pewter pitchers made after 1920, worth
$25–$45

Pewter plates in background, if old and marked, **$125**. Potbellied mug on left side, **$40–$60**. Hot-water bottle in foreground, **$85**. Small teapot goes for between **$100** and **$200**, depending on the maker's mark on the bottom.

Pewter coffeepot with graceful spout, by John Dixon.
$150–$175

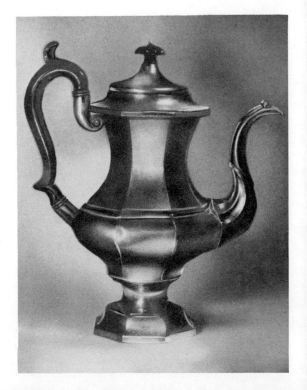

Unmarked communion flagon, 13 inches tall.
$300

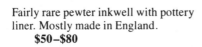

Fairly rare pewter inkwell with pottery liner. Mostly made in England.
$50–$80

Crown-handled porringer or soup bowl about 5 inches in diameter. Unmarked ones sell for between **$75** and **$150**. Marked ones run **$200–$300**.

Phonographs

Oak tabletop Victrola with label inside cover.
$150

Old Edison with morning-glory-type horn. Around **$400** for this one.

Graphophone with short brass horn.
Desirable size.
$175

RCA Victor table model with little
white dog on the horn. Depending on
condition,
$250–$350

Fluted horn, table model.
$250

Group of horns that are often used alone as interior decorations. The morning-glory horn in the center is the star—**$75–$85**. The others, **$25–$35**.

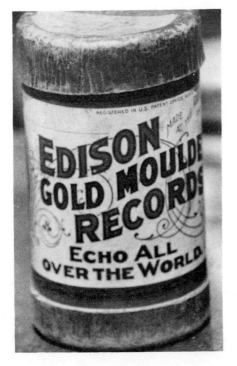

Music box with 14-inch discs are very sought after. Brass punched discs, painted scene in cover. They range from **$300–$1,200**, depending on size and number of discs that come with them. This one is **$350** with only one disc. Discs are worth **$35** each.

Original cylinder records can be purchased for from **$5–$10** each. Includes carton.

Edison Home Phonograph with cover lettering in good condition.
$300

Photographic

Daguerreotype.
$50

Long undervalued, daguerreotypes are coming into their own. This one has leather case with cut-velvet interior, pressed-brass oval. **$75** and climbing.

A close-up of the kind of character that built America.

This is an example of the kind of daguerreotype you can still buy for **$45** because they are priced by insensitive clods who have no appreciation whatsoever of the content of the pictures. This is a historic work of photographic art that should sell for **$500** or more, and soon will.

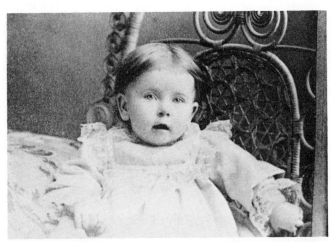

Studio portrait of a Victorian child born with a silver spoon in its mouth.
$40

Family portrait album. Victorian.
$150

High school or finishing school photo of some refined young ladies.
$15

Close-up of one refined young lady. Much remains to be done with these old photos using present-day photographic technology.

Small studio portrait of a Southern belle from Louisiana in 1922. Such photographs that have character are still way undervalued at
$5–$10

Still shots for movies that used to be displayed in glass boxes in theater lobbies. Now available at **$1** each. Just begging for selective collection.

212

Portrait vase of Bristol glass with photograph transferred onto it.
$45–$55

Bristol-glass beaker for holding toothbrushes in the bathroom with photographs transferred onto it by lithophane process.
$15

Plates

Shards of ironstone china found in the sandy beaches of New England where the old wharves for whaling ships used to stand in the early 1800s. Broken dishes were just thrown overboard. So whaling men certainly ate from these plates. **$1** apiece.

A very attractive Delft oyster set—English china from the early 1900s. **$150** and up for a set of eight, depending on how quaintly decorated.

Dedham pottery with typical orange rooster, black outlines, and cracked glaze. Also rabbits and lobsters, whales, butterflies. English.
   $125–$150

214

Historical blue china showing landing of the Pilgrims; made for American Centennial.
$150

Deep-blue Staffordshire china. Stags and does, late 1800s.
$100

Rose O'Neill Kewpie-doll plate, very sought after by doll collectors.
$75–$100

Booth's china with little bluebird-of-happiness decoration. **$10** each; premium for sets.

Highly glazed German pierced plate with pair of cherubs. Dessert plate **$25**

English biscuit set—cake plate and tea cup and saucer.
$75

216

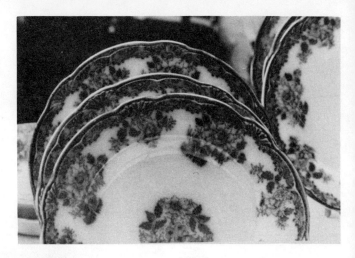

Decorated blue ironstone ware—no flowing. Booth's, early 1900s. Plates **$10** each.

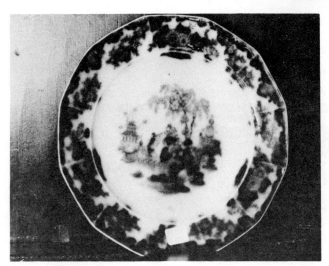

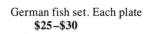

Real flow-blue like this one runs **$45–$60** per plate.

German fish set. Each plate **$25–$30**

217

Multicolored German bonbon dish.
hand-painted before it was glazed.
$65–$75

Open-work souvenir plate with decal
face.
$25

218

Prints

Gouache illustration for a magazine of the period. On academy board.
$200

Print of *Killing of the Sacred Buffalo*. Hand-colored lithograph. Late 1800s, **$150**. A few rare Currier & Ives ones dealing with Indians are up in the **$1,000s**.

Popular Victorian print in gold-leaf frame.
$35

N. Currier lithograph that sells for **$75**. Several price guides for all Currier & Ives prints are commonly available at your local antique dealer's shop.

Framed print, hand-colored, from a seed catalogue.
$40

Popular Victorian print for the game room or family bar.
$45

220

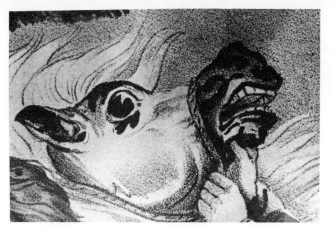

Close-up of horse on Currier print to show how drawing was established by black-ink lithography and coloring done by hand—in a production line system.

Close-up of signature on N. Currier print.

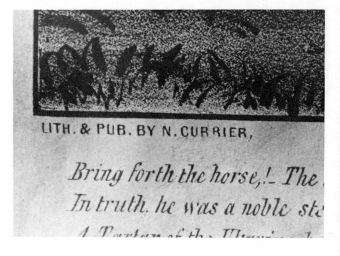

LITH. & PUB. BY N. CURRIER,

Bring forth the horse,!- The
In truth, he was a noble ste

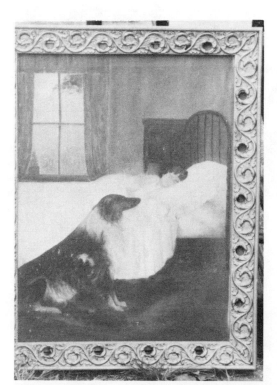

Print from the '20s in ornate frame.
$35

Evening Prayers is a hand-colored lithograph print slightly later than the Currier & Ives period.
$35

Full-color valentine printed in Germany on what were then the only eight-color lithograph presses in the world.
$20

Unframed print of the Dionne quintuplets, very collectible for the doll collectors and toy people—as well as a decorative conversation piece.
$35 or **$40**

Full-color lithographed print pasted on semi-cheesecloth and then mounted on a wedged stretcher to simulate an oil painting. Usually varnished, too. Called a chromolithograph. This one, **$25**. Best subjects go up to **$65**.

Safe at Home print dated 1876—the Centennial year. Even in its deterio- rated condition, this one is worth **$45**. A perfect one would be worth **$150**:

And this is an authentic Atwater Kent that sells to electronics afficionados for **$125**, though much higher is asked by many dealers in this sort of thing.

Antique radio speaker for your Atwater Kent. Still works.
$60

For the less electronically minded, a 1920s model table radio like this one goes for **$45–$75** if working without a hum.

Metal-cased speaker of good tone and some decorative value.
$35

224

Sewing

Sewing bird held ribbon, material you were working on—was a third hand. With pincushion, **$125** plus. (When you squeeze bird's tail, his mouth opens.) Screw attaches it to edge of table.

Dressmakers' forms, not very old, **$25**. Old ones on cast-iron bases are up to **$65**.

The Stay Stuck Pin Cube of dressmaker pins.
  $12

Two-drawer thread-spool cabinet. Everybody wants one, so even only two drawers fetch
$150–$200

Spool chest full of shallow sliding shelves.
$175–$225

Spool of thread holder and sewing box, quite rare.
$110

Salt and pepper set. Pickard mark on the bottom. Baked-on hazy golden finish. The set,
$75

Imitation of the Pickard line sells for only **$20** the set.

Japanese-made souvenir set.
$10–$15

Silver

Cigarette box with monogram, 6 inches wide, lined with mahogany as a humidor.
$50–$85

Sterling silver napkin ring, **$40**. Plated, **$10**.

Sterling silver napkin ring with engraving and chasing around the middle.
$40 •

Plated silver napkin ring with ear of corn decoration, which people love.
$15

Sterling silver olive stickers with identifiable figures on each. The set,
$85

Footed sterling silver bowl about 4 inches across. Originally had glass liner for serving mustard or something.
$35

229

Fine luncheon set with pearl-handle knives, worth about **$10** for each piece.

Two coin-silver spoons, very thin, 80 percent silver. **$20–$25** apiece.

Bone-handled fish set of Victorian origin.
     $25

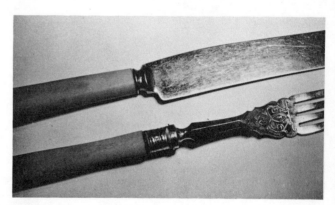

Sterling silver berry spoon.
     $30

Sterling silver serving pieces. Depending on degree of ornateness and size, **$35–$75**

Plated silver sugar and creamer with matching tray. Desirable hunt scene on sides.
$80

Occupational spoons showing the hunter, the cow, etc. Each **$40–$70**

Souvenir spoon of the Boston Tea Party. Sterling silver, **$25–$45**, depending on how near to "mint" condition it is.

Souvenir spoon from the land of the bean and the cod, where the Cabots speak only to Lodges, and the Lodges speak only to God. Sterling silver, **$30**

Six-piece plated silver tea set with matching tray from Victorian period. This one replated.
$400

Sterling silver tea ball.
$45

Sterling silver tea strainer. Here shown
upside down.
    $35

233

Smoking

Once you could buy Philip Morris cigarettes in this tin box with a sliding top.
Now **$10** for the box alone.

Meerschaum pipe in original fitted
case, **$65**. Some intricately carved sub-
jects go to **$200**.

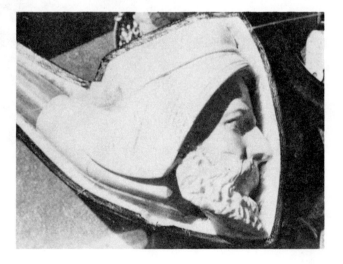

Meerschaum pipe with a lady on the
end.
    $75

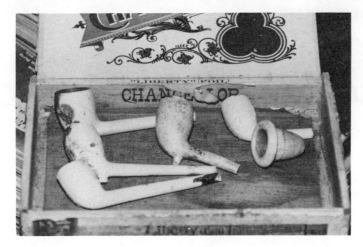

Collection of clay pipes. Each
$3

Clay pipe sold and given away by tobacco companies. Each
$25

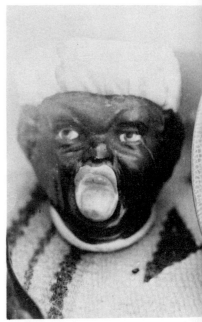

Burl walnut snuffbox with a hinged
cover, 4 inches long. Nice patina.
$30

Bright reds and greens and black and
gold make this 4-inch-long tobacco tin
worth
$12

235

Another 4-inch-long tobacco tin. Colorful yellow.
$12

Seven-inch-wide tobacco tin.
$24

Collection of tobacco tins running from
$10–$30

Antique basket and net used for trout fishing. About forty years old and about **$40** apiece.

Billiards scene on a wooden match case.
$25

Victorian oak bobsled—kid size—with wrought-iron runners. **$75–$150**, depending on condition and amount of decoration. This one only **$80**.

Autographed photograph of Babe Ruth and his wife—autographed by both.
$150

Commemorative poster of the 1903 American League champions.
$35

Jugglers' dumbbells, nice old paint and patina on the wood.
$45

Pair of Victorian barbells with painted stripes and nice patina.
$35

238

Memorial poster to the King of Swat.
$35

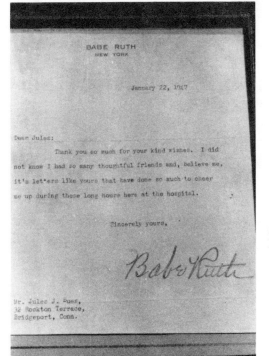

Standard answer to fan mail that the
Babe sent out. An autograph.
$150

Pair of wooden, strap-on ice skates
from the Victorian era.
$25

Statues

Eighteen-inch-high plaster statue of girl
with cat in the manner of Rogers, but
not one, but good, **$50**. If a Rogers,
there would be more than one figure and
would be worth **$200** for an average
one. Many worth a lot more.

Art Nouveau type of bust about 18
inches high.
$125

Alabaster of mother and child 2 feet
high.
$200

Bas-relief plaster-of-paris plaque 3 feet
wide, a casting of three ladies in the
Grecian manner.
$150

241

German stein of ordinary variety, 14 inches high.
$125–$175

Hunting scenes are most desirable on German steins with pewter flip caps like this one.
$125–$150

Add a dash of Breughel with these peasants dancing in the tavern, and you have another **$150** object. (Steins marked "Metlach" with a castle symbol are worth two or three times as much because of the workmanship and fine detail of the decoration.)

242

Common 2-gallon crock once found on
every farm. Stoneware.
$20

Freehand, joyously decorated 2-gallon
stoneware jug. Blue-gray with deer in
strong cobalt blue. Once corked
molasses jug. With this deer,
$175–$225

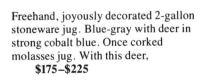

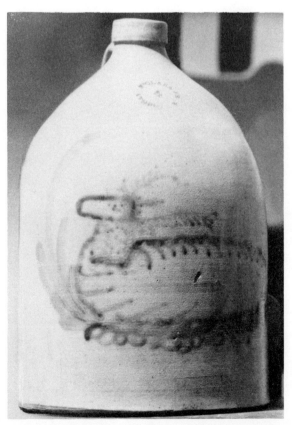

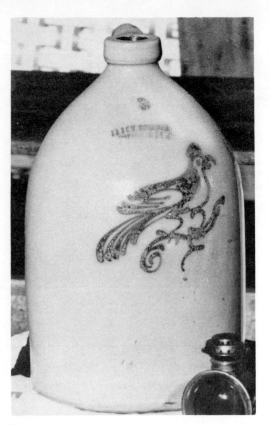

Underwood jug from Fort Edward, New York, has cobalt-blue decoration of a little bird in a tree stenciled onto it.
$175

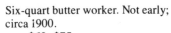

Six-quart butter worker. Not early; circa 1900.
$60–$75

Brown glaze stenciled on, another advertising jug. Grocer sold vinegar in it, charged you for jug, which you refilled.
$40

244

Picnic jug in brown stoneware given by a hat-making and -selling company to its customers in Albany, New York. Advertising item. Pewter spigot is missing. Nevertheless . . . **$35**. Double with spigot.

Detail of hatter's thermos jug

Stuffed Animals

Teddy bears are hot these days. If *antique*, selling from **$25–$200** depending on size and condition. Older ones have longer arms.

Here's a really old Teddy bear in a dress, going for
$90

Homely-looking bulldog.
$25

Nice little dogs that are just barely old enough to command around
$25

Victorian horse pull toy—12 inches high on wooden base and cast-iron wheels. Not rare, about
$75

Horse pull toy, **$75**. Wind-up tin toy,
$45

Later type of pull toy.
$35

Telephonics

Oak-cased wall telephone with writing shelf. Early model.
$200

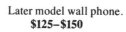

Later model wall phone.
$125–$150

First dial model standing telephone with lots of shiny brass, rare, **$125**. Early all-blacks are **$40**. The most recent of the all-blacks, **$15**.

Wall telephone with earphone on cord (not seen here).
$65

Upright phone of most ordinary type.
$25

Telegraph key, available for from **$40–$60**, depending on how much brass and if shined up.

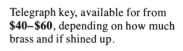

Tools

Double molding plane.
$30

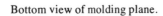 

Bottom view of molding plane.

Early brassbound bit brace made of mahogany, **$125**. Fancier ones go up to **$350**.

Detail of bit brace.

Block plane only 5 inches long.
$15

Toys

Giant nesting blocks—largest
one is a 14-inch cube.
$175

Toy typewriter.
$25

Small cast-lead toys running from
$7–$22 for the best little airplanes.

Three-foot-long fire engine. Metal toys
this large are rare and go for
$150–$200

Wood top spun with a string.
$3

German-made Noah's Ark of lithographed paper glued to thin wood
sheets, measures 20 inches long.
Hinged roof. Sells for **$45** without ani-
mals. Animals of carved wood are
$5–$25 each depending on intricacy of
carving and painting.

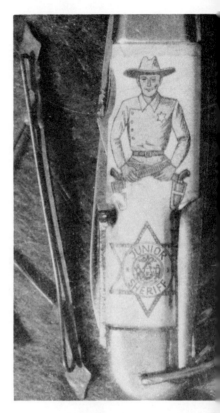

Child's penknife.
$12

Little girl's sewing machine that really
works.
$35

253

Rocking horse of carved wood.
$200

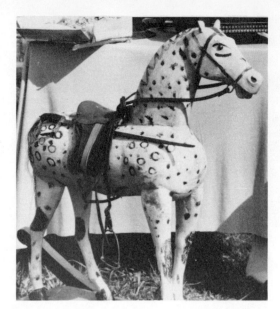

Lionel engine from the 1920s.
$75

Wood and cast-iron toy about a foot
long sells for
$65

Batman and Robin in futuristic auto
done in '50s.
$40

Tiny cowboy single-cap shooter.
$18

Standing kaleidoscope that looks down
at turntable on base. A fantastic Victorian toy that somebody should still be
making.
$45

Foot-long coupe with battery-operated
headlights.
$85

Hubley sheet-metal toy.
$20

1940s tin trailer truck worth
$40

Working early toy steam engine, 9
inches wide.
$150

Very fancy toy steam engine with brass
boiler, firebox, 18 inches long.
$450

Alcohol-burning toy steam engine with
lots of brass, 10 inches long.
$175

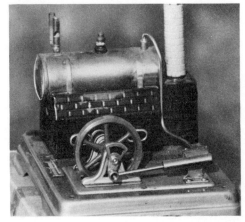

Toy cap pistols from
$5–$20

Cast-iron trolley car, even with rear wheels missing, is **$20**. With all wheels, **$40**.

Cast-iron railroad car, complete, but only remnants of original paint. **$50**

Four-inch-long Model T in cast iron, **$45**. With a lot better paint, **$75**.

Cast-iron school bus with a comparative lot of yellow paint still on it. **$45**

257

Nice roadster.
$40

Late cast-iron trailer truck pulling 1930
Model A roadsters. With the four original roadsters still on it, this is very rare.
Also paint is in very fine condition.
$650–$750

Cast-iron roadster with silvered pressed
wheels.
$35

Early but ubiquitous ice wagon.
$125

Early racing car with hardly any paint
left, but very rare.
$225

Dump truck with pressed-tin wheels.
Because dump trucks are rare,
$125

Gray Packard touring car.
$75

From the late 1930s, this sedan goes for
$18–$22

Trolley car with cast-iron wheels.
$45

Tin railroad engine. **$65**.(No works.)

Junky little cash register.
$20

Wind-up, bell-ringing Ferris wheel
from the 1940s.
$125

Grouping of railroad cars tipped on
their sides. Not old, **$7** each.

260

Mechanical billiards game in original box.
$250

Poolroom toy. Depending on condition, **$120–$200**

German-made lithographed tin fire engine with wind-up mechanism in fine condition. Runs 30 feet.
$175

Wind-up drummer soldier.
$45

In this wind-up toy Woodrow Wilson lifts up his hat and the parasol spins as this model of an electric car passes by. Depending on condition of paint, **$450–$650**

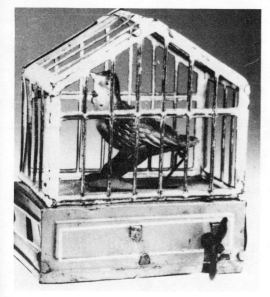

Bird moves back and forth while tiny bellows in bottom makes a whistle squeak. But so many were made that it sells for only **$40**

Bottom view of bird-in-cage toy. The bellows is at the right.

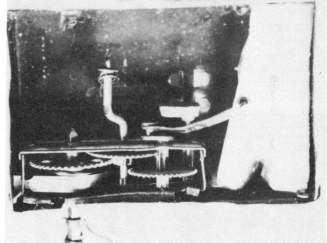

Mickey Mouse and Popeye command ridiculous prices. So these two lithographed tin plates and pitcher command **$75**. Amazing!

Farmer Brown wind-up toy 8 inches long, works well.
$125

Train runs through mountain, stops on signal; 4 inches wide.
$40

Beach sand pail is missing its tin shovel, but has nice artwork on sides.
$35

Typical French-made lithographed tin toy. Rolling wheels make the boy lean back and forth. Four inches long.
$65

Ugly little boy on a tricycle toy,
Japanese-made, sells to obviously
taste-free people for
$45

Tin wind-up Marx steamroller.
$75

English-style wind-up coach with brake
and real electric lights. A foot long.
$175

Tin wind-up farm tractor.
$65

Clown that walks on his hands, **$85**. An older version of this toy goes for from **$200–$250**.

Push-down top, old one.
 $45

English-made model auto, 16 inches long.
$250

Checker taxicab.
$325

Amos 'n' Andy taxi.
$650

Toonerville Trolley wind-up toy.
$375

Wind-up milk wagon from the 1930s.
$160

English-made double-decker bus.
$350

Weather Vanes

Cow weather vane complete with directionals, pressed-copper halves soldered together. Depending on patina and condition,
$450–$600

Nice design, copper weather vane, but bullet holes cut its value to
$150

Sports roadster weather vane, if original, **$1,400**. Even this reproduction is **$250**.

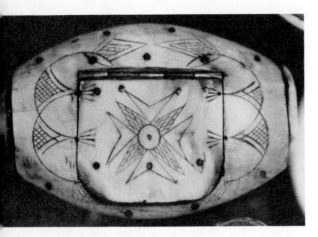

Scrimshaw hinged box made of bone, soot rubbed into incised lines. Four inches long. Snuffbox. Authentic.
$160

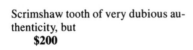

Scrimshaw tooth of very dubious authenticity, but
$200

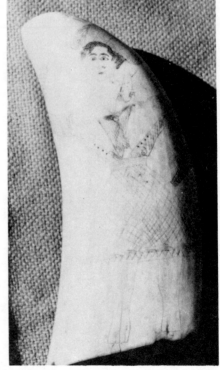

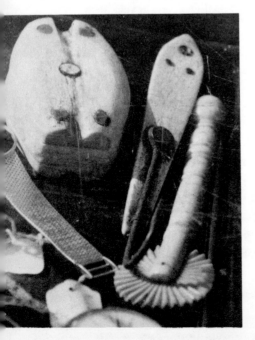

Whalebone pie crimper, **$125**; the pulley, **$50**.

Model of a whale made out of whale-bone.
$350

Professionally done oil-painting in-terpretation of the old whaling prints, probably done in the 1920s. This is a, detail.
$650

Victorian oil painting of whale hunting.
$1,200

Early whaling print, 20 inches wide, engraving, hand-colored. An excellent example of the genre.
$650

Wicker

Fancy wicker baby carriage with
parasol top in good condition. A winner.
$400

Very rare wicker vase, missing its glass
liner, but still worth
$125

Victorian wicker rocker.
$250–$300

Wicker table lamp and shade from 1920s.
$150

Wicker rocker.
$225